Stranger in his own Land

The Author

With all the expectations, dreams, desires and intentions he had, he found himself living a life he still had to detect the meaning of it. The prospect, as generally stated, of a black hole of nothingness once it came to an end did not add up to what he was looking for. Wasn't there more to it?

When searching for answers, he discovered outlooks much more promising.

The Essay

deals with messages of divine origin going back to what had been the crucial turning point in world's history. They were given about two centuries ago to a humble man devoting many years of his adult life to put them down in writing. Kept hidden at first, they were protected for a future when valued as the Lord's own genuine words, to be a light in the dark times ahead.

Stranger in his own Land

Past Times revisited

Produced and published by:
BoD - Books on Demand, Norderstedt

ISBN: 9783757886523

Content

Preface

2000 times and more the seasons turned since measuring time began and the years were counted, following the birth of a man like there never lived one before. In the past, people treasured his commemoration but today – who does know more of him than the mere name?

Known better, though, seems to be the Big Bang in the beginning which is said to have started it all, the existence of the universe. The way it was taught in school, it had to be taken for granted. But somewhen creeping doubt sneaked in: If it was Big Bang making the world, who in turn caused Big Bang?

By Big Bang, atoms were said to originate, banding together as material, specifically water, an ocean, in which all sorts of substances floated, developing into cells. The cells became amoeba which in progression were the great-grandmothers of all living things on Earth that crept and flew. Finally, out of it came the evolution of a real brain, able to meditate what to think about the matter.

Did one do so, thinking, there was this particular feeling that there must have been a fault in reasoning; something was missing! Or where was it to be seen that raw clusters of matter created warm and beautiful life out of themselves without a creator?

There were other tales, however, which began with the water and the ocean as well but then took a different turn: Everything at first being deserted and empty in a prevailing gloom, the report went on saying: „…and the Spirit of God moved upon the face of the waters."

God? A rumour of ancient times? Anything real? Once, so it seemed, people highly honoured him and the belief in him incited all cultural development, as if being its foundation. But now, when actually was the name to be heard last time? Had it been forgotten or even became a no-word, managing just a bare living in the shadowy interior of old churches? Was God a failure, whose son was known to have come to a bad end long time ago? If there was any reality to his purported almightiness, why had he not, given the known rebelliousness of a stubborn mankind, long since made short work of it?

According to older reports, though, this once did happen, known as the deluge, when the waters of the floodgates of the skies and from the abysses of the earth had washed away the dirt of a misdirected development. Only Noah, the Just, had survived in his ark, swimming into a better future.

There was a fresh beginning afterwards but that had been a long time ago. With reminiscences rather fading so many years after, another deluge seems to be due in the beat-up world of today. It does not necessarily have to be water, fire would do as well, the armoury of annihilation already being installed in many parts of the world. Alternatively, all sorts of flooding were feasible, microorganisms for instance, virtual or real, gone wild and out of control, wreaking havoc everywhere rumour had them to be.

The mystery of being – how to judge its essence independently from all freely offered academic insinuations? Does it make sense to read the original account oneself, the Holy Book, the Bible?

In older days, for such a demand, people were sent to the stakes and burned alive by the thousands and ten-thousands, ordered by the inquisition of an almighty church for crimes of heresy. Thinking for oneself was taboo on life's punishment, and for fifteen centuries the Bible was in a lockdown.

Today it's free as far as access to it is concerned, the New Testament being available to everyone. It contains the original four gospels, but difficulties might arise when trying to understand them in their compressed language. One might wish for upcoming questions to be answered more profoundly, suspecting that there is infinitely more to them than it appears at first sight.

Among the men and women, allowed a glance into divinity's spheres by grace of God, a man, Jakob Lorber, did live in Austria two centuries ago, where he was beckoned to serve as „God's Scribe Servant", faithfully to record what he received in words given by an inner voice. Living in utmost humbleness, Lorber, almost daily for 24 years in a row, continued his writings out of which, among other scriptures, emerged „The Great Gospel of John". After he died, his work was protected from being tracked and destroyed by the suspicious church. But eventually, the church losing its influence, it was edited by trusted friends and exists now as the full length recount of Jesus' three years walking on Earth, told by Jesus himself in his own wording.

Are they reminiscences from eternity? Gods gift to his own people – or were they, as non-believers claim, fantasies of a lunatic?

If one gets into it, many pages wait to be read – a challenge, a real rock of a book, consisting of roughly 5000 pages in small print, in eleven volumes. Be it one chapter after the other or pages picked at random – to an open mind each page might be a revelation, never in contradiction to New Testament's comparatively short text.

The messages cover a range a hundredfold wider in comparison to the gospels of the Bible, fully supporting the existing ones, to generate a broader understanding. To a reader who receives them without prejudice, the events, often given in full detail, more and more come to life.

The essence of the holy scripture widely being unknown, ignored, not taken seriously, even ridiculed – the reminder of it might be a guide to a forgotten truth.

1. Miracles

In times the counting of the years began, almost the entire known world was under the rule of the Roman Empire. Its sheer extension was immense and included Palestine, the Holy Land. The Romans, terminating endless controversies and fratricidal wars there, had installed a functioning administration which the former rulers had to conform with, a theocracy of the Pharisees and learned elders of the scriptures, represented by the priesthood of the Temple in Jerusalem.

They only grudgingly might have accepted the rule of the Romans, but what really upset them beyond compare was this vagabond roaming the countryside, Jesus of Nazareth, producing his cheep feats with which he allegedly made the blind seeing and the lame going, causing rebellion among the plain dumb folks believing it. Even if there was some reality in the incoming reports, the only way they could have been performed were fiendish manipulations, for neither was the troublemaker known to be a scholar of their own breed nor as someone being of any significance.

What made things much worse was his pretension to be the Son of God, and thus the Messiah, who, since times of old, was promised to arise.

Which was impossible because the Messiah was not imaginable as the shabby son of an old carpenter but as the mightiest king on Earth only, in the glory of an erected shining kingdom for his people. That was the reason Jesus, a stranger in his own land, was persecuted for three years. But until the end, when he surrendered to his enemies out of his own free will, they never got hold of him.

At times, he stayed in places under Roman jurisdiction, not belonging to the sphere of influence of the persecutors. As if called by an inner voice, educated people of Greek and Roman culture met there, doctors, scholars, executives, officers and businessmen. They often had lost faith in the old polytheisms, fetishes of wood and clay representing some Jupiter or Apollo as alleged gods. Many of these men already had the inkling of the only one and true God, and it was Jesus bringing the message to them which the rulers of his own people constantly turned down as a blatant lie, substituting their once genuine belief in the traditions of Moses for new rules made by themselves.

The friendship with the Romans reached back to the time of his birth in Bethlehem. It had been Cornelius, brother of the High Commissioner Cyrenius, ruler over half of Asia and Africa, who as a commander was stationed there to supervise the population census ordered by Rome's emperor. In this function, he met Joseph and Mary, the parents, and was deeply moved by the mystery surrounding them. He had seen the marvel of the incarnation of the godly child at close range and did what he could to help the family along. He saw the humble visit of the Shepherds and the arrival of the Three Kings from the wide ranges of Asia, and the inconceivable disaster sparked by it.

Because shortly afterwards he was confronted with the excessive ravages of King Herod, a local ruler, installed by the Romans under conditions of being a righteous governor. But Herod, fearing the newborn rival when the rumours reached him, turned out to be the opposite, ordering the slaughter of every male infant in the vicinity. The worst excesses of the infamous child murder Cornelius was able to prevent but could not ward them off entirely. As a result, brutal murder was carried out, killing five thousand innocent children.

But the Holy Family itself he was able to protect and safeguard them to the residence of his brother Cyrenius at the seaport of Tyrus. From there, paying a state visit to Egypt by ship, Cyrenius took them along to their exile. He cared for their adequate accommodation and, whenever his state affairs did allow, spent his time with them. He, one of the highest representatives of the Roman Empire, sensed the true ruler of the world in little boy Jesus.

Due to time-consuming duties of governing in a tumultuous world, Cyrenius eventually lost track of the godly child's family but 30 years later the recollection of the encounter made him, his brother Cornelius and other high ranking Romans presume who in the country it was, arousing such a sensation. And this presumption that it was the grown-up Jesus was confirmed when finally they met again.

As men of highest education, many Romans already recognized the truth of Old Testament's religious traditions but ever anew they were repelled by the fanaticism of the priestly caste of the Temple and their wicked laws, oppressing the populace and amassing riches and power for themselves.

Some words might be said about Virgin Mary, Mother of God, as they are told in the Gospel of Jacobus, also written down by Jakob Lorber by grace of the inner voice.

As a little child Mary had been given to the Temple in Jerusalem where she grew up as a „Virgin of the Temple" to the age of fourteen. Then she had to leave the place to be married to a man in due time. Prior to it, Mary was to be accommodated in some congenial household and cared for in chastity and decency. One of the qualified hosts-to-be was Joseph, a direct descendent of King David, even if being a simple carpenter only and an old man, long since widowed. In his modest household his already grown up sons were living.

It was him the task of catering for Mary was assigned to by ordeal. It stirred some confusion, least not with Joseph himself, fearing to be ridiculed by all the young men of the country which had gone to great efforts in this matter themselves. But the ordeal had been distinct. Among the candidates, standing in a circle, it was Joseph a consecrated dove had flown to and settled upon his head, indicating he was the chosen. Even if frustration spread among the others, Mary was given to him in trust.

There, living at his small property, she received Angel Gabriel's annunciation of the conception and birth of Jesus. When in due time her pregnancy became obvious, Joseph made the most bitter accusations because of her unfaithfulness, until he, by her fierce affirmation of her innocence and the appearance of the angel to him as well, realized his suspicion's baselessness. Yet, from the Temple, the worst was to be feared.

There the matter became known by an offended fancier of Mary. She and Joseph were summoned to stand trial in the Temple's court of the High Priests in Jerusalem, being accused of fornication, the most execrable sin, to be sanctioned by capital punishment. They were sentenced to death by drinking the poisonous „Cursed Water".

Thereafter, three days passed and to everyone's amazement the alleged sinners were not found dead with bloated bellies and torn guts but alive and cheerful. The priests were utmost puzzled and astonished. But they had to acknowledge the fact and let the offenders go free. In punishment of their suspected but unverifiable offence, however, Joseph and Mary were sentenced to orderly being married to each other. Which, on their part, made them praise and thank God for his graciousness and salvation.

Encountering Jesus, people were confronted with experiences they were at a loss to interpret them except as miracles. The gospels are listing some of them: Water transformed into wine, a crowd of thousands fed with a few loafs of bread and some fish, the sick and the crippled healed simultaneously by the hundreds and the dead resurrected. Generations of bible critics, in later times, tried hard to explain them away. But as long as the Holy Scripture in its richness does not get lost they stand for themselves as they did happen .

But, were they anything special? The Lord, Creator of Heaven and Earth in all of eternity, undoubtedly was able to create not only some but countless scores of miracles. Unless he, too, was explained away by the critics.

He, the initiator of the miracles, begged the two disciples skilled in writing, Matthew and John, which accompanied him when travelling, not to record them or at least only little of it because accounts of miracles did not possess any specific sustainability.

Witnesses of miracles the gospels describe went down on their knees in amazement and awe but those being absent, not seeing them with their own eyes, tended not to believe, shrugging off talks of them as fairy-tales. Miracles were only to baffle people, Jesus said.

Unbelievers had their minds boggled when confronted with miracles they inwardly were not ready to except as facts of divine origin. They had to recognize them, yet unendingly brooded over the way they possibly were effectuated.

Beyond them however, were the words of truth in timeless validity, even beauty. They possessed the quality to stay alive and present forever while solitary incidents like miracles were fading memories in the flight of time, less and less remembered when the years went by, until they were not more but faraway legends to those born afterwards, to be believed or not believed.

What really spoke to the hearts were the words of eternal truth. Only they had the potential to be remembered lovingly forever and form adamant convictions.

For people in dire need, however, to relieve their misery, to heal illnesses, still hunger and console sorrow, Jesus surely did let happen a great number miracles, as shown in the Great Gospel of John.

At times they were allowed in public as eye-openers, their performance being delegated to a helper of juvenile appearance. People not knowing him sometimes called him a milksop, first to grow a beard before talking to respectable men. At closer contact, they revised their assessment and preferred not to get too near to him but stay at a safe distance.

By approval of Jesus, for unbelieving contemporaries he transformed rocks into nothing or nothing into rocks. Or into bread. Once he did so into a big fish, which lashing about with his tail fin so vigorously it threw his new owner onto his back and a stronger man had to struggle to drag it into a water basin. At a similar occasion it was a real donkey out of nothing and the new owner of it was so horror-stricken he immediately passed it on to someone else although the gain would have proven favourable to him.

The helper's true nature, though, was a shooting star of unbearable brightness, whizzing through the skies with the speed of lightning. He had to enwrap himself in shadows to make his presence tolerable to men. It was an angel.

To demonstrate more of it, the angel, as if time did not exist in his world, whisked to remote places in Africa or India in the wink of an eye to bring back specific objects of the region. Same he did from the bottom of the sea. He transformed dry deserts into blossoming orchards or rebuilt crumbling ruins of ancient palaces to new splendour.

Once when a group of peaceful citizens was molested by an hostile military squad, two angels looking like frail adolescents made the soldiers spin around like feathers and even had their weapons to disappear, until finally they just stood there perplexed and aghast, mouth open.

Which could happen to friendly readers of the reports as well. But if ceasing reading prematurely, something substantial might be missed.

Accompanying Jesus to places under Roman administration, the said angel, by the name of Rafael, was asked to show his skill as well, converting the invisible into matter and let matter be converted into spiritual substance, his own body included. Open minded attendees were invited to check his hands and arms. Everything was in place to be touched at: skin and muscles, flesh and bones.

One moment later they were requested to do the same again – and it was nothingness only they grabbed. They reached through the body without sensing any resistance while Rafael continued to stand in front of them with a smile about their consternation. It was enough to make them revise their views of the world.

To them, it was the beginning of a new era and they wished for answers to the many questions they had. Rafael did his best to respond to their queries: Neither on the planet nor in the vastness of the universe, he said, anything like empty space existed, the alleged nothingness being light and energy everywhere, invisible to human eyes though. It was „Ether", matter not yet awakened, flowing through the world as a source of unending power. Out of it, specific matter of any kind could be created by mental force, or led back to its former invisible status within no time.

Rafael demonstrated whatever was asked for. But for all the power he was exerting he called himself the least servant of his Lord only, among countless scores of other angels.

Although it does not go along with official narratives, evidence of this kind of energy is discovered worldwide in experimental backyard workshops, where they try to exploit it commercially as a source of new energy, technically useable. But to reveal its spiritual dimensions widely still seems to be a task of the future.

When confronted with the issue, high-ranking physicists were not willing to comment on the subject, anxious not to destroy their reputation. On the other hand, they were not happy with their self-created definitions of matter and energy by which the universe can not really be explained. They still are in search for it and Rafael would not be the least able to help them along if he be taken seriously. Which, to non-believers, probably is a thought of absurdity.

More than once Jesus was hard-pressed by his followers to allow miracles in the presence of the Temple's High Priests, to finally get them convinced of his divinity. The answer was a flat No. Religious fanaticism of its worst kind was not overcome that way. Acts of divine origin would be defamed and vilified as black magic, performed in fiendish collaboration with Satan himself. It was to be abhorred and rejected in all of eternity.

2.   Lacking Gratefulness

After the return from Egypt Jesus lived with his family in Nazareth, a life seemingly in no way impressive. Grown up, he was employed as a carpenter in his stepfather Joseph's workshop for many years. Everyone in town knew him, without really knowing anything about him. He was considered a good and accurate worker but, for the rest, close-lipped and withdrawn.

Joseph, when asked about it, also had no better answer. As a little child, Jesus had shown many wondrous capabilities and was able to speak already shortly after his birth, amazing people by remarks of deep wisdom. But later on all of it seemed gotten lost until hardly anybody remembered it except Mary, his mother, and his family. Some in town even believed him mentally retarded.

Then, when he was thirty years old, after being baptized in river Jordan, his divine nature all of a sudden began to show. The news quickly spread but were not hailed everywhere, especially not in the vicinity of the synagogue, his immediate neighbourhood. There they were full of black suspicion, the Pharisees, the elders of the synagogue and the learned of the scriptures. A simple, unlearned carpenter stood up against them? Them, the representatives of the lore of thousands of years, from Prime Father Abraham onwards to Moses and Elias and, successively, to the High Priests in Jerusalem.

Provided, there was any truth to the incoming reports at all, it was presumed this sly old fox Joseph, in one way or the other, had his son sent to some obscure black magicians. They might have shown him feats and dirty tricks to rope the dumb folk into believing them. Whatever it was, everywhere this irritating talk sprang up about miraculous healing.

After a journey to Jerusalem, and an ensuing stay in the country of Samaria, Jesus returned to his hometown Nazareth. Because an affront of him in the capital's temple, stirring uneasiness when publicly getting to be known, the priests were anything but in a friendly mood. Yet, with a shock, they had to accept that one of their own respected associates, the principal of a nearby synagogue, Jairus, in an act of desperation ran up to Jesus begging and pleading on his knees to have his fatally ill daughter, dearest in the world to him, healed. Jesus agreed.

Their encounter remained not undetected and an enormous crowd gathered. In the jostle they only grindingly won their way. Before they were able to reach the house of Jairus the girl had died.

Due to old traditions the crying, moaning and paid singing of the laments began right after death. Seeing all the turmoil, Jesus demanded every screecher to leave the house, the girl being asleep only.

Which was met by jeer and mockery: What sort of a queerish sleep was it to be, when the body already grew cold and colourless and not the slightest trace of life left in the eyes? The yelling even increased until finally Jesus himself had to help to throw the bawlers out.

The scene ended, as described in New Testament, with the daughter coming to life again. An impressive instalment, however, is added in the Great Gospel of John as documented in one of its chapters:

The incident stirred up a hornet's nest and the girl's awakening to life led to an unheard-of bashing of Jairus. Facts forgotten, it was said that the daughter merely had been seemingly dead. She even, so the rumour went, might only have pretended dying to uncover the finespun lies of the trickster, definitely to get up afterwards and being fine. Jesus, the big dazzler and quackster – that was the smearing, spread about everywhere. Concerning its origin, a guess relating it to the synagogue probably wasn't wide of the mark.

To Jairus, things were getting precarious. He was forced to sign an official document that he had fallen prey to obnoxious fraud, otherwise he was to see his entire existence ruined and his civic liberties taken away. He signed, to outwardly remain a great principal while inwardly he felt like being a miserable traitor.

Hardly awoken to full life again, Sarah, the daughter, after she had been allowed a glance into the realms of heaven, fell into a deep depression over so much evilness and was ailing anew. It did not take long that she, merely a shadow of herself, lay on her deathbed again. Meanwhile Jesus, for his part, went away to counsel Roman officials trying to uncover a devastating crime, committed by not yet identified villains.

Jairus, principal of his home-town's synagogue, almost tore himself apart in pain and self-reproach. In direst need, he urged his servants to seek, whatever the road or place, for Jesus to beg him to help a second time. After an extensive search high and low they finally found him, yet were not even allowed to talk to him but were sent home with a short message: For all the piled up lies, Jairus might look elsewhere in matters of his private affairs!

In desperation, all high-ranking physicians were summoned in big haste, yet at the ill girl's bed, nothing came out of it but the confession of their total incapability. One of the medics though, Borus, from days together in early childhood a close friend of Jesus, could have helped but did not, hurling the truth of their treachery into the faces of the attending Pharisees and elders. For which they were to kill him and tear him to pieces, right on the spot.

The attack cold-bloodedly was warded off by displaying a little bottle from which, if opened, a poisonous vapour was to emerge, deadly to everyone except to himself who knew the antidote.

Borus, without further being molested, left the place and Sarah died. The heartbroken father had the body brought to a burial vault, accessible to visitors of condolence. There the officials of the synagogue were given ample opportunity to convince themselves of her definite death. Though after a couple of days they had to keep their noses shut for the decomposing body's smell.

Jairus, the father, fell into an abyss of self-reproach and feelings of guilt. He saw the splendid life he could afford grace to his high position, and the lies and dishonesty behind. He was aware of the potential to satisfy any wish in life he could think of and, at the same time, the crushing waves devouring him should he ever dare not to float with the tide.

„But think of the furious sensation this move may cause", he answered when Borus, son of a neighbouring wealthy family, urged him no longer to trample divine truth under foot as a high servant of God. Whereupon Borus had left, with somewhat uncourtly remarks about the matter.

Yet, after days of brooding, the good in Jairus, in commemoration of his beloved daughter, won its way in his inner struggle and conflict. He decided to renounce his splendid reputation and, if it must be, resign and step down from all official positions.

After this mental metamorphosis, Jesus, perceiving all thoughts from afar, had him called by an inner voice. Together with a local Roman official they went to the burial vault without allowing any other witnesses. Jairus fell on his knees, weeping and asking forgiveness for his wrongdoing.

Needless to say, Sarah's second awakening from

death resulted in the girl's deepest feelings of gratitude and an overwhelming joy of her parents at their reunion.

Jesus demanded silence to be kept about the incident. On a Shabbat-day, the hallowed day, he went to the synagogue where the Pharisees and elders were assembled as usual to study the books of old. By chance, the pages opened referred to verses of Jesaja, one of their highly honoured prophets, although nobody liked being reminded that Jesaja disgracefully had been murdered by their forefathers for bluntly voicing outright truth too often; which, as an aside, had been the fate of most other prophets as well.

The verses read were about desisting from sin, to refrain from evil by doing the good and righteous and help the oppressed, especially widows and orphans. When passages followed about thieves and defectors the elders grumbled why the book must have been opened just at this specific paragraph. But discussing the matter, they asked what actual meaning might be behind it, yet came to no conclusion.

Then Jesus stepped right up among them. „What are you musing at which as clear as the sun of high noon is in the presence of your eyes?", he called out. The addressed flew in anger, yet were forced to listen that, shamefully, they themselves were practising the opposite of what they were reading. Did they not rob helpless widows of their properties, ruining their existence? Wasn't it that they not only did not protect the orphans but had them sold as slaves abroad, condemning them to a life of misery?

What about the unfortunate children detained by slave traders in clandestine companionship with the synagogue, imprisoned in their dungeons until sold? And Mother Mary, what happened to her after her husband Joseph died? Disgracefully she had been driven from her little home when the Templars grabbed it for themselves.

Mary, though, was under divine protection and for everything wrested away from her she amply was compensated. But for others, injustice committed was screaming to heaven. The felons, blind to deeds of Jesus no living man on Earth was able to do, were confronted with their villainy when asked what signs and miracles were needed till they finally would open their eyes!?

In raging wrath the elders and Pharisees jumped to their feet, jelling: „You seedy beggar, what is all your arguing with us about! What signs and miracles are you talking of?!"

Secretly brought to the synagogue by Jesus, in the shadows of the background and not noticed by anybody so far, Sarah was standing. Now he took her by the hand, placed her right in the middle of them and asked: „Do you recognize this maiden? Don't you see what happened to her again?"

All of them were stunned and dumbfounded. Whisperingly, they asked each other how that possibly could be. They themselves had attended her funeral and now the girl was right there! Still in her burial gown but very, very alive.

„Now", Jesus said, „what is your evil heart saying? Is this sign sufficient enough or not?"

The proceedings sound like springing up from a nightmare: The elders, recovering from their shock, declared the incident an extraordinary sample of black magic, produced by hell and all its demons. They fiercely rejected the reality of it, for not to be weighed as sinners themselves by giving it any credit. Jesus, the wretch, they had known for almost thirty years might perform his tricks some way or other but it meant nothing but blatant deception to them.

Perceiving all this wickedness, Sarah cried out: „Lord, I beg you, let's get away from these crooked creatures. Near them I feel like Satan is standing right in front of us." This, and Jesus' answer, let the situation spin completely out of control. The infuriated, tearing their garment apart, screamed: „Away with you!"

What that meant, unmistakably became obvious when they reached out for the stones. The stones! They existed in every synagogue as well as in the temple in Jerusalem to enhance respect to the laws of religion. The Romans had granted the Templars a regime of self-determination in matters of religion to administer law and order themselves, resulting in stoning to death wrongdoers of alleged sacred commandments. The victims drew their last dying breath in a hail of stones next to the holy walls.

Blinded by fierce rage, the synagogue's leaders grabbed their stones and dear Sarah would have been well-advised to step aside not to die a third time, had it not been for her saviour. A whiff from Jesus would have let the stones crumble to dust or even turn the enraged into lifeless rocks themselves never to move. But that was not his intention, for the souls of the wretched might have been frightened out of their bodies never to find back.

Events took a different turn instead. The door of the hall suddenly swung open and in came a group of Roman officials, ahead of them – Cyrenius. The stone-throwers, all in a moment, hardly knew how fast and deep they wanted to bow down to the highest commissioner of Asia, well-known to them for his demand to strictly abide the laws.

When they discovered tears of joy in Cyrenius' eyes, finding Jesus after so many years, greeting him with words of warm cordiality, their colour changed to deathly paleness and they began to shiver as in an attack of fever, fearing Jesus to take revenge and lay open all their evilness.

Especially when they heard that the High Commissioner was on his way to investigate in matters of a vicious crime of unprecedented brazenness that had caused severe troubles to the Romans. To Cyrenius' utmost gratefulness the coup had been uncovered and the Templars were scared to death for their part of having been clandestine accomplices.

Despite his great joy, Cyrenius quickly sensed

something awkward going on but the evil's degree he only comprehended when Sarah, out of her agitated heart, gave a full report, setting his mind ablaze with anger. He threatened the principals of the synagogue to have the flesh whipped off their bones. But while they horribly began to whine, he asked Jesus under his breath which punishment to apply in reality.

Jesus was satisfied to have the culprits sentenced to everlasting silence concerning the incident, and never again say a word against him, else the said punishment inevitably be executed; Cyrenius, as Supreme Judge would look to it personally and it was well known he was not joking.

Whether the perverted servants of God were put onto the right track by the verdict, remained open but at least they had their mouths shut. Jesus, though, left his home-town never to come back.

3. Purge of a Temple

The crime Cyrenius extremely was distressed about could have inflicted immense damage to the country had it not been for the local authorities' reconnaissance that they eventually were able to uncover the plot. Hints given by Jesus had been quite helpful to get them on the track of it.

Executed by means of cunning intelligence rather than brute force, it was conducted by a faction of Templars without the knowledge of their superiors. The revenue payments of the whole of Asia, due to be sent to the emperor in Rome, had gotten lost, a caravan of several hundred pack animals loaded with gold and jewellery and other values. The affair could have led to an unprecedented eruption of Rome's rage, a devastating military invasion turning the country upside down and leave it in shambles. Luckily, the treasuries were secured in time and the offenders arrested.

To execute the fierce action they had disguised themselves as high-ranking Roman officials, one of them even as the venerable old Cyrenius. Being of authoritative appearance, exhibiting the Emperor's Ring and Golden Sword, ultimate symbols of power, though imitations, they had waited for the imperial caravan's arrival from the vast ranges of Asia.

Surrounded by associates, masquerading as Roman soldiers, they managed to identify themselves to the commander of the caravan's accompanying squadron as legitimate receivers of the transport, to take over and escort it further to Rome.

After the handover, the caravan disappeared in wide, inaccessible mountain regions. Secret trails, thought to be untraceable, had been build there before, leading to hidden places and caverns. But proceedings did not add up to the villains' expectations: Reaching their destination, they were waited for by officials and a military unit. By Roman standards, death was the only adequate punishment for a crime of such degree.

As it turned out, other felonies simultaneously were committed as well. Hundreds of young boys and girls were added to the shipment, kidnapped in the back-country by orders of certain Templars running profitable businesses of their own. The children were tied half nakedly to the pack-animals to be sent to the slave markets.

By the officials Jesus, for his part in thwarting the plot, was asked to render a verdict. But he didn't – knowing well that his intervention was not needed for the villains to meet their fate: The coup was conducted without the sanction of the High Priests. The fact itself would not have burdened their conscience but the pouring of immense riches into pockets other than their own was an unpardonable sin to be punished once and for all.

For the rest of their days, the wrongdoers would

be given ample opportunity to meditate their action – buried and rotting in the dungeons of the Temple. All the Romans had to do, was to properly ship them over, advising their elders to keep a better eye on their member's activities in the future.

The plot successfully foiled, everyone's dearest concern was to free the children, catering for their needs and re-clothe them, and to trace the where-abouts of the grieving parents to whom they were returned to their great joy.

Justice was done, for the time being. But in other cases helpless children had to endure nameless misery. Was it the Lord's task to constantly be on the watch to prevent atrocities? Was the name of „man" not to be earned by own efforts of them, in loving devotion to those never to see the light of the day by themselves nor surviving without tender care and charity?

Charity, and peaceful cooperation when living together, was demanded by Jesus again and again. If getting hit on the one cheek in a quarrel, be pre-pared for a slap on the other rather than retaliate, he said in the Sermon on the Mount, Math. 5,39. The thought required quite a deal of good will to get used to, but it still might be better than to start never ending fighting.

The disciples, at an occasion, asked: „Lord, do we really have to stand deliberate mistreatment by others, and suffering?" He answered: „Lo and be-hold for your doubting! For how long do I have to endure you!?" A phrase the disciples now and than had to swallow when they forgot previously given explanations or did not put them into the context they belonged to.

Living together in peace in communities was crucial by any means – as said in the commandment: Love your neighbour as you love yourself! It did not suit grown-ups to fight over what, in the end, might be nothing but a trifle. When someone started quarrelling, it was not specifically helpful to pay him out in his own coin. Even if words of conciliation were not honoured it would be better to try forgiveness. Not once or even seven times, but Jesus said: seven times seventy times!

It referred to life in communities where everyone knew each other and broken solidarity threatened the existence of the whole. Damage would be less if treasured rights were renounced for once. Thinking twice if given time, opponents even might become friends in the long run. If not, all of them might find themselves to be at the side of the losers.

Contrary to it, the dealing with tyrants and criminals was another chapter when they reckoned to get away with whatever misdeed and atrocity. Like when crocked characters of a misguided education get access to power as it must have been in King Herod's case. In his younger days, maybe he had better intentions but he never might have been shown his limits. Until, in vile excesses, he turned out to be the human monster, forever commemorated for his crimes. The only love to him would have been tough-minded force to prevent further atrocities.

A statement by Jesus proves he never advocated peacekeeping at any cost: „I did not come to bring you peace but the sword", he said – not a foul compromise but to stand up unconditionally for truth and righteousness. The way he himself lived on Earth was a constant confirmation of it.

In short wording, New Testament mentions the purge of the Temple in Jerusalem when Jesus expelled all merchants and dealers. The Great Gospel of John shows the details: The Temple was rented out for money by the greedy priesthood.

During the celebration of Passah, highest religious festivity of the year, the faithful flocked into Jerusalem by the ten-thousands from all over the country to do their prayers in holy contemplation as requested by religion. But by then, the Temple was turned into a huge marketplace, especially of animals. The holy halls, right to the remotest spots, were occupied by cattle, sheep, poultry and other livestock, dirt and excrements being everywhere. On long tables butchering was done, blood was flowing like water and guts piled up to heaps. Sickening stench all over the place, as well as deafening noise. Devotional souls, as far as not having fainted yet, had a hart time doing their prayers in worship of God.

Additionally, it was a romping place for thieves and robbers, and a visitor could consider himself lucky loosing his belongings only and not his life as well. But to the Temple's elders it always was the bargain of the year.

Jesus ordered cords to be brought, braided a whip, forced his way into the middle of the turmoil and shouted with a mighty voice: „My house is a house of prayer but you make it a house of stinking evilness!" The Temple was build to worship God and never to be sold out!

Bad luck for his opponents that they did not take him seriously but screeched and jeered. When the whip got into action, divine power was revealed, inflicting unbearable pain on bawlers and outbursts of blind fury on animals. Terrible yelling arose, cattle stampeding in wild panic, trampling to the ground what was in their way, causing vendors and buyers to run for their lives.

Scores of moneychangers conducting business fled helter-skelter, abandoning everything they had, their tables toppling over and the money rolling on the ground.

Jesus did not win friends among them by the action but he priests, on their part, were too busy to ponder much over what happened. In a frenzy they, servants and all available hands included, picked up the abandoned cash from the ground to put it into their own pockets. Records listed one thousand bags of gold, additionally streaming into the Temple's treasure chambers that day.

It was only later, that an argument arose between

the elders and Jesus but nobody dared to openly act against him. Instead, they tried to get him caught by cleverly devised arguments, but he read their faces and went away.

The incident apparently did not display much of love and forgiveness. But the only love the Templars knew anyway, was love for themselves in unconditional surrender of others. Which not exactly was what the Lord had come for to incarnate on Earth.

Afterwards, in the Temple, they in earnest started brooding over how to get rid of the unwelcome magician. That he could be more than that was beyond their comprehension.

Doubtlessly Jesus, exerting divine power, could have annihilated the Temple and its associates by a mere breath. But that was not his intention. Mankind was to be given the chance to reach the highest heights and the deepest depth, to experience the essence of good and evil in their extremest conditions. Everyone was to decide for himself on which side to participate in the creation. That was a promise and a right conceded even to the vilest adversaries. Both roads were open, and had to stay open, forever.

In response of the outrageous intrusion into their own spheres, the priests opted for brute force, preparing for retaliatory strikes. An army of thousand well-armed mercenaries was sent forth. At Lake Genezareth, the Sea of Galilee, they mounted an armada of ships in search of the rebel against law and order, from the shores to the inland. They got into a dreadful storm, drifted towards a coast of murderous cliffs, and perished. Survivors were to be counted by the fingers of one hand.

But Jesus, did he not say: Love your enemies!? A thousand of them were hanging suspended in the cliffs their ships were shattered against, bones rotting and falling prey to wild beasts. Who had it been to let the storm break loose? The record doesn't say, just that it happened the way it did.

It obviously was meant as a warning but the message remained unheard. Attempts to get rid of the rabble-rouser continued, yet, given the waste of manpower, not always another thousand men were available to do so.

4.   Spectacular Healing

Throughout the country, what most stirred sensations was the healing. Flocking in droves, people were bringing the sick and disabled ones. Their ailment's cause was manifold, results of a perverted lifestyle by their parents or by themselves, or poisonous evaporation from the ground or deficiency symptoms of half-starvation in bitter poverty when even the most needed was lacking. Turning trustfully to Jesus, many were healed and mysteriously strengthened.

As it happened to the woman of the Bible, bleeding for twelve years. She only dared to touch the seam of Jesus' garment from behind in a crowd of people, and she was well the same moment. He, the healer, had turned around and said: „Your faith bestead you."

Yet, not everybody was healed since illnesses served as means of correction of erroneous ways of life. Restored health soon was wrecked anew when insight was lacking and life went on as before in craving for lust and pleasure. That was the reason why Jesus lovingly turned to many of the sick, healing them, while passing by others without taking notice.

On occasions, hundreds of sick and crippled

were brought, being sane all in one moment. But when, without own efforts of the healed to change their ways of living health did not prevail, it was grist to the mills of the enviers and grudgers, eagerly blazoning out Jesus as a quack and charlatan. Especially the Templars did so, embittered that people turned their backs on them and spurned their petitionary prayers so dear to be paid for.

Scoff and scorn caused some of the ailing to give credit to their accusations and abstain from coming to Jesus. The awakening was bitter when the healed ones jubilantly returned and the ill stayed behind in misery. They only could be helped when sincerely altering their attitudes.

Though reluctantly, the opponents had to admit the reality of the healing but were pondering how to get profit out of it for themselves. Once, they turned to Jesus asking about a patch of land blessed by him to effect healing of the ill which were brought even when he was not present – would it unfurl its marvellous potential in the future as well?

The blunt answer given was that they had nothing else in mind but to seize the property by their financial power, solidly fence it in and charge mighty big entrance fees from those seeking healing. It definitely would not have been in favour of the ill but all the more so of themselves.

Ever since days of old, illness was a most profitable source of income. So-called medics, bragging and fumbling about at bedsides, were keeping patients just above dying with dubious drugs and mixtures while asking for hefty fees. When the sick died anyway, the lemon squeezed out to the last, they walked away, shoulders shrugging.

Jesus advised them never to show up again unless they wanted to taste his divine wrath. Many diseases and their fatal outcome would have been unnecessary had the patients been allowed rest and recreation right from the beginning in an atmosphere of love and attention instead of suffering dubious treatments.

Enduring their pain, the sick patiently waited until they got healed. But most spectacular events happened as well and became widely known in the region, stirring up amazement and excitement. Like the healing of the two maniacs near the town of Gadara, at the eastern coast of the Sea of Galilee. The gospels of the Bible give a short report of it while the incident is described in full detail in the Great Gospel of John.

The maniacs were the cause of fear and horror of the entire region. They were living at a mountainside cemetery opposite Gadara, screaming, rampaging and horrendously hurling lumps of rock against each other. They were naked and ferocious to a degree nobody dared to stay near the place or use the main access road to the town. As if the furious were in contact with the demons of the gruesome tombs, they seemed to get their superhuman strength from them.

There had been attempts to tame them. In a weary hour, they once were overwhelmed by a squad of the strongest men and shackled with heavy chains of iron. But it was in vain. Regaining strength, the maniacs tore the chains apart like thin thread and the rampaging went on day and night with terribly distorted faces. Watching from afar, nobody wished to ever get in their way.

But when Jesus came it all changed. They rushed up, fell down to his feet and screamed at the top of their lungs. It was a screaming not deriving from the maniacs themselves but from the demons inhabiting them. Sensing a force infinitely mightier than theirs, they feared the end of their misdoings had come. They cried to Jesus not to increase their agony by taking away their dwellings inside the maniacs' bodies.

Being commanded to instantly leave their prey, they had to obey, metamorphosing to vast numbers of big black flies buzzing through the air. Yet, they beseechingly carried on pleading for not being driven out from the region entirely. Their plea was granted in a very strange way:

The profession of the region's inhabitants was raising pigs; eating pork not being forbidden by their pagan religion. Selling it far and wide to fanciers was their flourishing trade. A big herd of the animals was grazing nearby.

Open to their request, Jesus allowed the demons to whisk into the pigs. These, in turn, went mad and furiously ran to a high mountain cliff stretching far out into the Sea of Galilee. There, from three hundred feet above, they went tumbling down into the waters below where it was deepest, drowning themselves all in a moment. Two thousand by the number! The herders were horror-stricken.

The owners in town, confronted with the news, were shocked as well, unendingly speculating what the cause might have been. The most probable explanation to them was the vengeance of the gods. If not of the mighty Zeus' himself, then at least of the great Neptune's. Due to insufficient worshipping, supposedly.

It was decided to immediately invoke and urgently beg the gods not to cause further calamities, but never to mention the damage suffered for not to provoke more of divine wrath. The residents set off to go and look out for them.

Some foreign bystanders, however, voiced a different opinion: The alleged Neptune probably being nobody but the notorious Magician of Nazareth! But to get rid of him as fast as possible, likewise seemed to be the best option.

Arriving at the place of the incident, the owners of the pigs were baffled not to find a raging and vengeful god but the group of the disciples and their quite human looking master. Even stranger to them was the sight of the two former maniacs, neatly clad now, their faces shining with joy when giving the recount of their salvation.

The residents, their only worry being not to get into troubles again, could not figure out what to think of it. So they, with all due respect, asked no further questions but begged the whimsical strangers would they, please, leave their town? Not wanting to disturb anyone any longer, the disciples readied their ship for departure.

While doing so, the two healed ones rushed up, desperately pleading not to be left behind but taken along as members of the disciples fellowship, be it even as their lowest servants. Looking back at their lives, they feared to be spurned everywhere and turned away in horror, scorned until the end of their days.

But Jesus had different settlements in mind. He send them out all over East Jordan as his witnesses to testify for him and his mission. Whatever hardship they were to endure, he promised to be with them in spirit and strengthen them when needed. In times ahead, they gave their testimony and many, plain folk and the better situated alike, were won to become true believers of the new faith.

Due to healing and preaching in public as in the Sermon on the Mount, Jesus' fame widely spread. So much so, finally thousands followed to the places the rumour had him going, beleaguering the houses he supposedly was to stay. At times, there was no way to enter or leave them but by a secret rear-entrance.

Eight brothers came, carrying a bedstead in which one of their kin was laying, suffering from gout, limbs withered and joints terribly distorted, unable to the slightest move. Hastening to the place the great healer was said to stay, they found the house surrounded by a vast crowd with no chance of getting through.

The brothers approached the owner they were acquainted with. For the time being, he had no better information than that the house inside was overcrowded with folks as well. Additionally, many Pharisees, priests and elders had squeezed in, claiming their right to observe strange occurrences on the spot which they were entitled to.

So the proprietor offered a different solution: The roof being covered with reed, it partly could be removed if necessary to open access to the attic from the outside. There, by a trapdoor, the interior could be reached.

To the cheering of the crowd the attempt was staged. A fussy Templar, apparently not having found a place inside, complained about violation of Shabbat regulations and called it sin. In return, one of the brothers called him an old temple-oxen and, being on the roll, added further remarks cheered by the people even more.

When they were ready for the descent through the trapdoor, a sharp-voiced inquiry came from beneath what it was, going on up there? Instead of an answer, the bed, held by four ropes, was floating down, with comments the priests considered highly disrespectful. But by ducking their heads down below, they definitely had to give way to the bed.

Weeping and pleading for help, there the cripple was laying. Jesus recognised his trust and his true faith. He said: „Be comforted, my son, your sins are forgiven!" As a sheer blasphemy to them, the words immediately triggered complaints by the elders of the synagogue. If anyone, only they themselves were the ones authorized to forgive sins by divine grace, provided it was paid for appropriately! This beggar Jesus – what did he think he was?

Not all of the Pharisees thought alike, though. Several of them well remembered Sarah's awakening from death which had made them wondering and change their minds. But they only were the minority.

Jesus asked, whether health could be restored by solely talking about forgiving sins, unsupported by divine blessing? His opponents scoffed it off: Regardless of any idle talk, the totally crippled figure in front of them never was to be helped except in one way – by death!

What followed is described in the Gospel of Matthew when Jesus said: „Stand up, take your bed and go home!" In amazement, everyone gazed at the miserably shrivelled and twisted limbs of the sick when straightening and becoming wholesome in one moment. The flesh came back and so did physical strength. Crying with joy, the man got up, jubilantly thanking the Lord and, shouldering his bed, forced his way through the gasping crowd which loudly began to praise and laud God.

Left behind were some very hard thinking elders of the synagogue, wondering how ever to keep going on with the old hostility towards Jesus.

5.   Wolves in Disguise

The nuisance of the healing continued. To arrest the villain at any cost pursuers were sent out by the Temple, sly as wolves in sheep's clothing. Large-scale actions having failed so far, smaller units were to accomplish the task which if bluntly called by its real name was: Assassination! The instruction was: Him – dead or alive! If alive, the rest was to be taken care of.

Outwardly, the bloodhounds camouflaged as devout servants of God, eager to hook up with the looked for to learn about his preachings. Jesus let them find him but, unfortunately, often in areas of Roman jurisdiction where the pious servants of the Temple did not think it a bright idea to draw murder weapons from under their pilgrims disguise with military personal lingering about.

The way things ran was not very smooth, anyway. Did the pursuers try to spy on Jesus' whereabouts they went astray. Did he allow to be found they sometimes stood right there without recognizing him. Did he show his identity, they soon realized they were in the wrong place when authoritatively trying to accuse him of rebellion against the Temple by their cleverly devised arguments.

Jesus perceived all their secret thoughts. But instead of fending off the pursuers right away he rather embarrassed them by pointing to quotations of the holy scriptures, prophetically speaking of his coming and unjust persecution. When, just the same, they tried to get hold of him he mysteriously disappeared, to their ever-growing frustration.

The disciples wondered why the ruler of the world was fleeing and hiding like a thieve in the night. He did so out of mercy upon his adversaries. It was not really helpful to have them damaged or killed in action in their furious pursuit, not if it could be prevented. Even to them who were sent to murder him, the chance was to be given to come to their senses. The commandment „Love your fellow men like you love yourself", was to be applied to them, too, whenever feasible.

But above all was the demand to love God as the Creator who unendingly loved his creation. If it was not for him, bountiful life was to end in decline and annihilation. Men going astray in their aberration had to return, be it even after ages of time, if they wanted to continue living. In the long run, life was not granted without love for the giver of life, the Creator.

Yet, love never was to be enforced. No-one ever would be deprived of his own free will, the essence of his being. Everything done must be achieved by one's own will and insight.

Jesus occasionally went to desert regions east of River Jordan visiting forgotten villages nobody knew.

Nobody except the tax collectors of King Herod, the secular power of the country beside the Temple.

Herod was entitled to collect taxes by the Romans which knew, the excruciating murder of five thousand infants not being forgotten, their associate's evil nature but felt bound to treaties already in existence. The old Herod severely had paid for his atrocities by slowly being eaten up by horridly spawning lice until he died. But his successor, another King Herod, was not in the least better. His tax collectors, bloodsuckers as they were, tortured the people at will. The peasants, in their dried-out country, hardly knew what to make a living from, let alone pay taxes, often increased to a degree of absurdity.

Without mercy their livestock was taken away, the last sheep or cattle driven off by blackguards even if the animals were skin and bones only. In search of anything usable, the roofs of their miserable shacks were torn down. If that added up to nothing, the villagers garb was ripped off their bodies and their children and young women were seized to be sold at slave-markets on the Mediterranean coast. The Romans issued strict laws against such atrocities but their courts were far away. Complaints did not make it to the authorities, or did so only in rare cases, too late for harm already done.

Jesus and his disciples visited the region to help its dwellers in their misery, miraculously providing the necessities they needed to carry on.

At times, the disciples were sent out to conduct

missions of their own, after having received the gift to help and heal and prevent injustice. Once, just about in time, they came to a village Herod's blackguards were wreaking havoc, ripping apart the places of the tattered residents. Nothing found of any value, they snatched their children, tied them up and threw them onto a waggon to haul them away as their loot, leaving behind the families in nameless misery.

One of the disciples, Peter, stepped forward and demanded an immediate halt, threatening the pack's leader with heaven's retaliation. The thug, as an answer, drew his sword, ready to strike while scornfully swearing. That was the end of him. The scoundrel was struck by a flash of fire, bursting out of the ground below, burning him to ashes right on the spot. The other villains, limbs trembling all over, vowed never again in their lives to commit atrocities, pleading on their knees for mercy.

As it turned out, some of them later-on stayed with the disciples as their helpers with the task assigned to them of spreading the gospel, becoming true believers themselves of the new messages.

In addition to Herod's plague, people suffered from all sort of diseases. Gout crippled them, leprosy left them rotting alive, demons obsessed them in a state of permanent mania, and of the blind ones, the deaf and the lame, there were more than enough.

Jesus helped wherever he went to. Not before long, the places he stayed became well known when masses of the populace were bringing their sick ones. Sometimes hundreds of them arrived at the same time and were bedded under open sky on a field until their saviour came. By a word and a gesture of blessing he healed them all in a single moment. Finally, there were thousands following anew to the places he stayed.

But it was not healing alone they sought. They hoped for Jesus' messages too, which were so much different from the Temple's self-declared laws which served their crooked religious policies only, twisting and blurring the commandments given by Moses.

Events like the Sermon on the Mount did happen in several places where huge crowds held out for days without food. But ultimately their hunger had to be stilled. A few loaves of bread, wondrously augmenting, fed thousands of them right there and a great deal of leftovers was collected for further supply.

The activities could not be concealed from the local priests which were obliged to report them to the Temple in Jerusalem. In disguise, they sneaked up to the gatherings and mingled with the people. Jesus spotted them in the crowd and, while giving his teachings, he embarrassed them by openly addressing their treachery. Being outnumbered, they did not dare any hostility.

But in due time they, in detail, transmitted their observations to the Templars who ever the more were brooding over feasible ways to get done away with the impertinent magician.

Whenever a spark of goodwill seemed to be left, Jesus tried to win his opponents over to the path of truth, even if radical measures be applied.

Travelling the country, he and his disciples once were blocked by the local priesthood when entering a town. Identified as the well-known troublemakers, they were suspected to spread seditious speech to the public. Not willing to consider any reasonable argument, the priest's temper heated up and voices got louder until they began to use force to drag the would-be intruders to the municipal judge. Mocking Jesus' alleged divine power, they sneered whether he would show them a sample of it, please?

Their wishes were granted faster than they ever thought. Next to every ravager, all in a moment, stood a snarling lion. Incidentally, the nearest lion fit as a watch keeper over wrongdoers would have been down south on the African planes, many days of travelling away. But now, here they were, fourteen by the number. A growl at the slightest move was sufficient to convince the adversaries keeping quiet would be the better option. Without further molestation, the pilgrims, late as the day was, casually strode through the town-gate.

With other odd occurrences happening too, the residents had to reconsider their attitudes when confronted by the messages the strangers were bringing. Meanwhile, the arrested outside the gate went through a complete transformation of their minds, feeling the paws of the beasts at their necks to tear them to pieces any moment. It was some hours later only that they were freed, when their beseeching pleas to pledge good will had been transmitted to Jesus by spectators.

Realizing for how long they had lived in mental darkness, their leader, formerly the most ferocious of the infuriated, tried to explain their erstwhile aggressiveness: All their lifetime they had trusted the Temple's doctrine of the coming Messiah to be a shining hero and invincible avenger to all their enemies. When, instead, a plain carpenter arose, a simple working hand at the construction sites of his equally simple father Joseph – it did not match at all their conception of glory and magnificence.

When this plain carpenter began preaching, calling the Temple a place of evil, they could not but join the hateful chorus of their superiors, especially since the Temple's income diminished by thousands of pounds of gold. The dazzler, as Jesus was seen, by displaying his tricks and inexplicable healing, turned away the masses of the people on behalf of his own benefits.

The priests, as subordinates rank and file only compared to the High Priests with their unlimited power, had to howl with the wolves, condemning the impertinent trickster whenever there was the occasion.

Everything a High Priest said was to be taken as a law. Did he declare two times two being five, then it had to be this way. Did he determine the sun being black, then it was black, absolutely. Those with opposite opinions were marked for special treatment to develop a more adequate attitude, provided they survived the 'cure'.

The converted, now that they knew better, vowed never again to engage in actions against Jesus, whose real nature was revealed to them. But they hardly would be able, they said, to convince their many still blind co-priests of the same truth.

Jesus foresaw them in times to come to be hardworking labourers for his cause, giving testimony of his divinity throughout the country. Much hardship and persecution would lay ahead of them but they were promised to be helped whenever it was needed, never to be left alone as trustful followers of their Lord.

6. Unloved Duty Escaped

For their own good, Jesus wished his pursuers to come to their senses before too much harm be done. Some, inwardly, were opposed to their duty right from the beginning but kept it hidden for fear of prosecution. But even when acting as outspoken hardliners, they had to think twice when suffering themselves the evilness they inflicted on others.

Thirty of them, young temple-folks, were on the move by ship on the Sea of Galilee. In a sudden gale, the waves rose higher and higher until they were in danger of sinking. The ship, half a wreck of a rotten barge, the only one they had managed to find when continuing their journey, started falling apart, leaving the travellers screaming for help at the top of their lungs in the darkness of the middle of the night.

Jesus, staying at a place of his Roman friends, drew their attention to the impending disaster threatening the group. Despite some snappish remarks of no major damage be done should this kind of contemporaries serve as fodder for the dear fish, a life raft was readied. Valiantly the rescuers rode the heaving waves, caught up with the shipwrecked just in time and safely brought them to the shore.

The newly arrived were embarrassed to find that

it was a Roman fortification they had come to. For caution's sake, they inquired for the costs of the emergency rescue, a question they never would have asked their own folks. For everybody was expected to feel highly honoured to participate in rescuing the servants of God even if they drowned themselves when trying. But with the Romans, to be on the safe side, the Templars rather checked.

Mark, fisherman and ships' owner, a respected former Roman soldier and resident of the place, waved that off. Rescuing people for filthy money was not the custom with him. Quite the contrary to them themselves – he could not help to remark – charging big fees for rendering even the smallest services.

As it was with their petitionary prayers they as highest servants were authorized to forward to God on behalf of those seeking help. Afterwards they left the petitioners financially ruined by exorbitant fees. Needless to say, all of it was mere blubbering, totally useless. Thus addressed, the young folk looked even more embarrassed and the whole question was idle anyway, because they were almost broke.

They confessed that inwardly they no longer consented to the Temple but any insubordination would be sanctioned by severe punishment, imposed not only on them but likewise on their kinship. Listening to similar admissions not for the first time, Mark understood their troubles. He understood as well that they were nearly starved. So he offered to look for something to eat even when they said they would not know how to pay for it. Mark waved that aside too.

Spotting a merry fellowship, seated nearby and engaged in lively conversation, the newcomers, out of curiosity, inquired about them and were told they were a circle of friends of the places' Roman commander. Hearing his name, the inquirers grew pale, their hearts sinking into their boots. Remembering an encounter with this very officer, they only now sensed where they really had gotten to.

As a matter of fact, they already had been to the place before when sent out in search for trouble-maker Jesus by order of the Temple. Getting into what they thought to be a mere guest-house, they arrogantly had demanded free board and lodging, humble services included, which as emissaries of the Temple they were entitled to. Bad luck to them, that they had come to the military area of a Roman garrison not to be entered without a special permission. Could they produce it?

The temple-folk had boastfully denied, being liable only to God and the Temple but to nobody else. The commander, Julius by the name, held a different opinion and ordered to make short work with them. They had to pay hefty fines and further-on, according to the rules, they as intruders were to be bound and put into custody, to be transported to a special location, their eyes and ears sealed with paste of clay.

Which was executed as ordered. Never in their lives, the Pharisee offspring was to get near such a devilish tyrant again and now they were right there anew and in a fix. They ducked and hoped not to be recognized for they still lacked the appropriate travel permission. The Temple had considered it unnecessary if only they were to act big enough.

Mark perceived their uneasiness but, nevertheless, invited them to the place. He assured them that the party was benevolent folk, nothing to be feared.

The newly arrived were served with whatever was left at such a late hour. Everything dished up being welcome, the guests heartily helped themselves and, spirits rising after emptying cups of wine – the best they ever had, they said – their tongues loosened. Encouraged to speak out freely, they talked about the misery they were entangled: They had to swim along in the Temple's mainstream, grand institution of deceit. Rather today than tomorrow they'd turn their backs on it if only there was a way out.

Talking about their adventures while dining, they mentioned the encounter with the Roman commander. By chance, they were overheard at the company's tables and one of the listeners came over, seated himself next to the newcomers and friendly inquired about details. It was Julius whom they did not recognize. Though suffering his humiliating orders, they had not met him personally.

Bold by then, they dished the dirt of how disgustingly they had been treated, worse than a wild beast. Their listener, in return, raised concern over this dreadful Julius' orders and asked if he possibly might have been more accessible had they not acted so arrogantly at arrival?

They could not deny it but had done so because they always had been taught behaving this way was a downright privilege of them, the servants of the Temple. Priests and their offspring were to be served humbly by the rest of mankind.

Seeing the point now, they regretted, definitely deciding to alter their lives and get done with the duty forced on them. Their big question was how to escape, fearing the Cursed Water, the Temple's prevalent means to crush insubordination, the deadly bane of poison that was said to bring guilt or innocence to the light of the day.

If guilty, the poison was to rip the accused offender's guts apart, leaving him miserably to perish. If innocent, it was left to the Almighty to hold a protecting hand over the suspect. But, with the exception of a very remarkable and special case already mentioned, it had not happened for generations and the thirty young Pharisees were not inclined to rely on such a heavenly favour.

As little toddlers already, they had been given to the Temple by their status-seeking parents. In due time, when grown-up, they were given the choice of becoming spies and assassins in its service or to possibly savour the Cursed Water one day. They chose the former but it did not turn out too well, as the incident with Julius had shown, who still sat at the table asking for more details of the story.

When Julius finally revealed who he really was,

demanding their confession that they were set to track down Jesus like bloodhounds, they were seized by horror. Were they to expect revenge and retaliation?

They stated that, while on reconnaissance, so many wondrous reports of the alleged agitator Jesus had come to their knowledge, they had ceased to believe the lies spread about him and never wanted to cause any harm.

Julius, treasuring sincere words, understood and put their minds at ease. As far as he was concerned, there was nothing to fear now. Additionally, he promised to help.

The problem was that the Temple viciously held the whole family liable for offences of its members. If any of them defied their assigned missions they were bound to by terrible oaths – or even fled the country for neutral territories – the turn was for parents and siblings to taste the Cursed Water. To fake being missed in action or lost in a disaster and considered being dead, was the better option but even that was no guarantee: There were many subtle ears in the Temple's service, eavesdropping on anything suspicious, at home and in far away countries alike.

What to do? Julius returned to the honourable companionship at the nearby tables. Among them were Jesus, Cyrenius and other high-ranking Romans. Discussing the situation, Julius, a determined servant and advocate of the law, had a problem with the solemn oaths which the youngsters had been forced to by pledging loyalty to the Temple. Should they be breached?

Jesus' statement was distinct: Oaths, enforced in violation of all human rights, were null and void! The Templars themselves breached their own oaths whenever it was suitable. To breach wicked oaths was no sin.

Cyrenius rendered his verdict without much hesitation: The temple-folk was to be arrested anew, this time for good! For repeated defiance of Roman laws and missing travel-documents. The verdict was to be sent to Jerusalem. There the families of the offenders were entitled to sue the Temple in Roman courts for compensation of the loss of their offspring, sentenced for offences while on duty.

For the time being, the young folk was to register with the Roman military until appropriate assignments be found within the vast Roman Empire, according to their proficiencies. Gifted with a new existence, the convicted were more than pleased with the verdict.

Allowed to stay with the company, meeting a host of other visitors from all over the empire, it was the beginning of the most exiting changes in their lives. New outlooks and experiences never even guessed before opened new horizons when invited to participate in the unfolding events of a transitioning world.

7.   Pardon vs. Damnation

The Temple's elite was exceedingly enraged by any
healing of the sick on Shabbat-days. All activities
were considered violations of the laws of Moses and
therefore a damnable crime. Though their interpretation of Moses' teachings hardly was in line with
reality, the priests declared that Satan himself had
free access to men's souls on Shabbat-days when
engaged in doing anything. Which never was to be
allowed, except by a certificate of exemption, issued
by them as topmost servants of God, in exchange
for profound donations of gold or other values to
their treasury.

At occasional encounters Jesus asked what to do
if an oxen or donkey fell into a well on Shabbat-day.
Kindly pull it out or wait till Shabbat ended the next
day? Due to circumstances, the animal might have
perished by then and its carcass would befoul the
well.

Inquiries of that sort were not very welcome.
Shabbat was Shabbat, to be observed in all strictness
without a twist of a finger done. Which actually was
the reason one of their cities, Caesarea Philippi, was
burned to the ground. The fire broke out on a
Shabbat-day and everybody stood by arms crossed;
no-one to be allowed fire fighting on grounds of

religious misconduct.

It were the mansions of the Pharisees, though, that went up in flames first. But their owners were quite confident to have reconstruction funded by the state treasury, for they were, after all, the representatives of the authority securing public order.

To this end, fifty of them set out to the nearby place the Roman Commander in Chief Cyrenius temporarily was residing, led by their grey-bearded major, smart and shrewd in every way. What they did not know was that Jesus secretly stayed there the same time. What they did not know either: In view of the blazing flames at the horizon, Cyrenius had sent for reports about the disaster's cause.

In a dismal mood, with assumptions of his own, he awaited the pious servants of God, well known to him from previous confrontations. In carefully chosen words he was addressed by them, elders of the synagogue, lamenting their ill fate and bringing forward in humbleness their request, in confident anticipation that their petition benevolently be granted.

Cyrenius, in contrast, had something else to say: Who, by hideous behaviour, had fanned the anger of the city's residents to such a degree it got out of control turning into open rebellion? With the result of a torched township and smouldering clouds blackening the sky. Inflamed with rage, fiery tempered hotheads had set the place on fire. Not enough that the riots were not quenched because of Shabbat, no measures were taken to extinguish the fire grace to their religious regulations.

The priests were deeply saddened by the sho-
cking defamation and the blame laid on them,
claiming they only had been led by purest motiva-
tions. Cyrenius, obtaining contrary data, more and
more was disgusted and felt like spitting nails.

The facts: The day had seen a solar eclipse. When
the sun disappeared, the people in their ignorance
were horror-stricken and, with strange spectacles
showing in the skies in addition, went mad in their
panic. Hurrying to the high servants of divinity,
they beseechingly begged for their advocacy to God
to have the world's imminent doom averted. To
their restricted knowledge there was no other way.

The priests though, very well being familiar with
the celestial phenomenon, seized the opportunity.
They fiercely preached about the sinning and evil-
doing of the plain folk, righteously being punished
for it. If anything, the ongoing disaster was to be
averted solely by the total sacrifice of their gold,
money and anything of value. Consequently, the
people ran to bring everything they had.

In town, though, some sober-minded, cool-hea-
ded residents still were left. They knew the correct
interpretation and spread their knowledge.

When the people woke up to the blunt reality the
vanishing of the sun was to be explained naturally
and eventually Sun was to reappear, they were
boiling with rage how perfidiously they had been
cheated out of their values. Full rebellion broke out,
leaving the town in ruins in the wake of it. Yet, the

Pharisees insisted on being innocent.

Cyrenius, on his part, inquired what they possibly would have done with all the extorted riches prior to the end of the world? Time to squander them by their luxurious lifestyle hardly would have been left.

Cold-bloodedly, the priests did not show signs of embarrassment. They cunningly argued that there was no other way to react lest the panic of the populace had risen to unpredictable dimensions. Accepting the values as ultimate sacrifices was the valve to let off steam of their overheated emotions. Besides, who was to prove that, after sensations had cooled down, they would not have given back everything?

The local attendees of the hearings choked, knowing the priest's blood-sucking mentality all to well. Give back anything? They, the Templars?

But those were not in a mood to engage in discussions whether they would have or have not but insisted on strict Roman laws to be applied, demanding incontestable evidence of guilt. There was none, so, they argued, they were not to blame, on no account!

Cyrenius knew the slyness of his adversaries and, by fast-riding messengers, ordered eyewitnesses from town to his residence for further strict examinations. Until their arrival, the suspects were to be arrested.

The priests increasingly grew uneasy, especially in view of dreadful atrocities, looting and murder, occurring in the wake of the insurrection. They themselves, just about in time, had made a bare escape.

The chief of the Pharisees, keeping his temper, produced his last and biggest trump. Out of a secret pocket he drew a document, provided with imperial seals, in which the emperor himself guaranteed absolute immunity to its holder. Any violations of these statements were to be treated as offences sanctioned by capital punishment.

The first moment Cyrenius was aghast, the document appeared to be genuine. The priests would have been unassailable. How, in all the world, could they have obtained the document? How did they convince the emperor of their unswerving loyalty? Were they really invulnerable?

In the background, being unrecognised so far, Jesus stood. Counselling Cyrenius, he identified the document as a falsification, fabricated with extraordinary skill and subtlety.

So it was game over for the priests. A felony of that dimension, faking imperial seals, was to be punished by death. Additionally, they disparagingly had voiced comments about a certain insurgent and rabble-rouser in the country. As they found out, Cyrenius held a total different view of it. Becoming aware of their blunder, the priests in horror dreaded the worst. They already saw their heads rolling off the chopping block.

Yet, things took an unexpected turn. Jesus, seeing the traces of decency in their younger days, prior to their minds being twisted by an excruciating education, forgave them. In their childhood, they had grown up under the Temple's surveillance and its dominant influence. Knowing the harsh consequences, protest against the rules had been out of question. Awareness of their own identity eventually corroding, they functioned as executors of their educators' evil will, becoming evil themselves by craving for wealth and power.

By human standards Jesus' patience of dealing with them hardly is to be prized. If a trace of sincerity still showed, he appealed to them to turn away from evil and put their mental abilities to better use than to the Temple's mischief. Return to morality though, after their eyes were opened, entirely had to be left to their free will's own efforts.

Lies and deceit laying bare, the priests saw the vanity of their previous values and were inclined to revise their attitudes, especially since they were haunted by feelings of guilt for the murder of their fellow-priest Zechariah, once committed at the altar by their leader, lasting heavily upon their minds even after many years.

Now that they were under the sway of the Romans, they made a general confession, honestly regretting what they had done, and voiced their desire to start a new life apart from the Temple – if they only knew how. Cyrenius, moved by their repentance, offered Roman citizenship to have them protected from persecution by their former rulers.

Others, rotten to the core with atrocities committed throughout the whole of their lives, were marked for different treatments when overstretching.

Boarding a ship together with the disciples, Jesus sailed the sea of Galilee, bound to a remote fisher-village hardly ever anyone came by, its dwellers living in utmost poverty. But they neither were especially unhappy nor did they feel deprived. Having travelled the world far and wide in times gone by, they were convinced to know all about Earth' vanities, its odds and ends, and did not expect anything substantial of life any more.

But surprised by the arrival of guests they were and, nevertheless, bade them a welcome. They gladly were to share everything they had, they said, which was fish. For the rest, there was not much to their avail for further service. Neither did they possess chairs and tables, nor dishes, knife and fork; all they had to offer was plain fish boiled in water and eaten with fingers as they themselves did, and that was it. Not even salt for seasoning.

Their actual question, though, was what the newcomers really had in mind, coming to their place. Did they have to hide for some obscure reason? Were they persecuted and on the run? Jesus denied but that was half of the truth only. He foresaw that the place would be the scene of an encounter and a day of reckoning long overdue.

The fisher who had welcomed the guests went inside his hut to prompt the cooking of the promised meal of fish, meagre as it was. But shortly afterwards he reappeared, wife and children trailing behind, beaming with joy. Where in the world did they had their eyes not having noticed that the strangers meanwhile secretly had equipped their house with a large supply of groceries? For a long time they'd be furnished now. Right away, the fisher ordered a special hearty meal to be prepared.

Things seemed to be very strange though to him. But his mind got completely unhinged when Jesus asked for a jug of fresh water and, when it was brought, let it become wine of the best sort. It was a phenomenon he could not bring in line with his life's experience.

While the cooking was on its way, the fisher nevertheless rolled out his philosophy of despising life's vanity: Nothing was to be feared and nothing hoped for either but death alone, gracefully liberating men from an existence they never had asked for, imposed on them by unknown dark forces. This alone being true bliss, hopes for more were pure illusions.

To argue him out of his stoical views, brought along from a stay in Greece where he picked up their widespread philosophy, John, the disciple, was assigned. Not before long they were engaged in hot discussions. Joining them, curious about the guest's intentions, neighbours of the fisherman showed up. Tough nuts to be cracked, John had a hard time to stand his ground against their arguments. But he asked them whether they never had heard of God in this place? Should there, in the long run, not exist a better prospect than death and blind fate alone?

Talks and discussions went on till late in the night. Miraculously, out of thin air, comfortable benches and tables had emerged and, when darkness set in, a bright lamp was shining atop the setting at the beach they were assembled.

The fishermen had to swallow a lot, not being in accord with their philosophy. But totally incredible to them was the mental ability of John to lay open every incident in the previous life of one of their comrades when he travelled to remote places in Egypt, and all his secret thoughts and feelings alike he had when being there. Very thought-provoking, indeed, it appeared to them; how on earth were innermost secrecies be known by others?

One of the men suddenly got up, eavesdropping into the night. Looming danger seemed to be ahead and prompted them to dim the light had Jesus not held them back. Strange sounds were heard from beyond the thicket of seaweed growing in the shallows by which the inlet was closed off against the open sea. Seafarers, not knowing the way, were bound to go astray in the maze and ran aground, but the approaching ship must have been piloted by helmsmen familiar to the place.

And it was closing in fast. Soon coarse voices rang out, shouting menacingly. The newcomers apparently were in search for this very specific place, at long last finding their prey they had looked for, odd ducks as they sneeringly called them, now comfortably sitting together in a row just to be grabbed. The order was to have them arrested without delay as suspected supporters of the country's troublemaker, providing him a hideout.

The moment the ship hit the shore, heavily armed warriors jumped onto the beach, ready to use brute force. Despite for all their unswerving stoicism, the villagers were not to wait for their doom but immediately dash off to secret hidings in the mountains of the back-country. But again, Jesus held them back, putting them at ease as he did when they demanded the dimming of the light.

The pursuers came on. Stepping up and facing them, Jesus begged for mercy and postponement. Rattling with chains to constrain the victims, the brute's answer was outrageous cursing. Arrest be executed, on the spot! No mercy whatsoever! Weapons drawn ready to murder at slightest signs of resistance, all pleas fell on deaf ears.

That was the end of them.

In the wink of an eye the aggressors became stiff like being frozen, seized by maddening pain. Screaming and wailing, they resorted to swear to high heaven they'd give in and do whatever was demanded. When their yelling increased, the fishermen almost could not bear it and even some of the disciples pleaded for mercy and pitifulness.

From surrounding mountains the phenomenal roar of big predators was heard and that was the mercy designated to those who themselves never in their lives had shown any traces of mercy, devils in human disguise as they were. As young ruffians, they already had been standing in the front row of those conducting Herod's abominable child-slaughter. Excruciating cruelties they had perpetrated, uncountable young children of both sexes they had raped and killed, throwing their flesh to the blood-hounds afterwards. If the poor parents dared to inquire the whereabouts of their offspring, it was the last to be seen of them as well. Abominable crimes a thousandfold – enough was enough!

When their screams got shriller ever the more, Jesus saw the villains to commit even worse atrocities if pardoned, their souls being beyond mending as long as they lived in their physical bodies.

Downhill the mountains, a host of tigers and bears leaped forwards, soon to be on the spot, snatching the villains in their jaws and carrying them away like sparrows. Thereafter, only the crunching of bones sounded through the night. When eventually it ceased, the meal was over and, for perpetual commemoration, the disciples had been shown a lesson by their Lord of quite a different nature from what they were used to.

The traitors, poor fishermen who had piloted the warship through the shallows for small fees, got away alive but they, too, were taught a lesson they never forgot as long as they lived.

The villagers, in later days, were summoned to leave the hidden place they lived to meet Jesus again, becoming hard working labourers for his cause over the years.

8. Why all the Misery?

Back then, same as today, the odd question did arise: Is there any proof of God's existence, given what happens on Earth? Instead of charity a world of hate and conflict, of poverty, hunger and misery, of wars and diseases. Quite the contrary, was it not downright proof of his non-existence? If there really was a creator, why had he not accomplished any-thing better by his creation?

Jesus, Son of God, who said he was one with his father – even his followers sometimes were befallen by lurking doubt while living and travelling with him. The atrocities of Herod, the misdeeds of the Temple – were there no thunderbolts left for the Lord to smash the culprits? No fire raining from the skies as it happened at Sodom and Gomorrah, the sinful cities? Why did he tolerate such blatant mischief?

The questions the disciples had erupted anew when they came across authentic reports of crimes crying out to heaven in their outrageous monstro-sities. Inhuman murder of five thousand infants in Bethlehem and vicinity still being remembered, the sacrifice of innumerable innocent children continu-ed in hidden places of evil, their blood taken in ritual murder and sorcerous rites of satanism.

Listening to the facts alone, known but sometimes concealed even by authorities, made people feel horridly sick .

Jesus replied it scarcely was but a faint whiff of what he saw and knew himself. Countless masses were declared heretics and cruelly put to death, whole populations were obliterated in brutal wars in the name of religion. Future evil, no less atrocious, was to continue when wars openly were fought in worship of Mammon, god of money, and the power granted by it.

Yet, it was part of divinity's greater scheme. In the long run, evil must destroy itself, no matter how high it raises its ugly head. „By now, you will not understand yet", Jesus said but the disciples doubted whether they ever would. They still pondered over why it all was allowed by God.

The question had been there consistently, reaching back to the time of Adam and Eve. In their paradise, why couldn't they have lived on happily forever in all of eternity, in heavenly joy? Legend has it that it was the serpent and the principle of evil coming into the world by it. It was the serpent to insinuate to the innocent paradise-dwellers to eat the forbidden fruit, the root of all further mischief: The not-yet-allowed apple of the Tree of Knowledge of Good and Evil.

Other historical traditions dug a bit deeper: The calamity not solely derived from the apple itself but from the way it was presented when Eve sat under the tree. With the suggestion how sweet it might be, the apple was laid into her lab by the serpent and when Adam followed the invitation to look for it, he found something in addition, and that was the end of heavenly innocence. He learnt about Eve's true nature and, consequently, passion originated.

The assumption hardly would be far from truth that only by this very experience they became real human beings. Short of that, they would have been bound to stay angel-like denizens of paradise forever.

Despite their bad conscience afterwards, the taste of the fruit might have been „sweet" like the serpent had promised. But since the apple came from the Tree of Knowledge, bitterness too was not far away. They had to learn about the necessity to distinguish between right and wrong, good and evil, and to take a firm stand. The consequences, not very long afterwards, showed within their own family when one brother was killed by the other, Abel by Cain.

Things getting out of control – could it not have been prevented by God, ensuring mankind to live on the sunny side of the world only and be spared all gloom and cruelty?

The issue continuously emerged at gatherings of the disciples or in meetings with high-ranking Roman officials when they visited Jesus, looking for solutions to the multiple problems they were confronted with. Touring their vast empire, reaching out to the remotest frontiers of the known world, they had seen many miseries and deficiencies when even the best-intended social legislation sometimes was not much of a help.

Besides, the Romans themselves, by conquering other countries, did not always proceed very delicately. But in doing so, they created the Pax Romana, the peace lasting for centuries in Roman controlled territories which before often had seen chaos alone and lawlessness among its many various tribes and races. After peace was installed within the boundaries of the Empire, travelling and trading was facilitated without threat to life and property. But even then chaos and violence were not controlled for good; peace and justice were to be fought for ever anew.

Living in peace and harmony in a sphere of love, beauty and kindness without the need to fight for it and distinguish between good and evil, never would have served true humanity's progress. To choose a life of striving for lovingness and charity or to sink to the abysses of evilness, was the price to be paid for to belong to humankind.

The choice was reserved to the dwellers of this very planet Earth only. They were permitted to live as they wished, and the freedom of choice had to be untouchable forever if they were to stay humans. This way, the noblest qualities could unfold, as well as most wicked aberrations. With no superior power standing by to interfere when going astray, correction was men's own task in following the divine call to reach out for heights unguessed before, as it was their true destination.

Yet, trees were not to grow high up to the skies infinitely. Everyone was free to act as he liked, but he had to bear the consequences of his deeds too, returning to him be it right away or after ages of time. Strokes of luck, joy or misery in life, accidents and ailment, success and achievement, were the results of deeds done or misdeed committed, returning in due time like a flock of homing birds.

Innocent suffering, inflicted by others, would be compensated on a different level. If facts were considered broad enough, existence was not confined to the narrow ranges of birth and death. With doors into the future to open, hardship lived through on Earth would be balanced during life's proceedings, in accordance with the everlasting divine truth.

Danger, when identified and necessary precautions be taken, could be dealt with. But war, famine and worldwide misery, condemning uncountable individuals to live or die in poverty and peril – was there no mercy of God at least for the children to let them go untroubled?

From a humanitarian point of view, the question seems to make sense. But was it God's duty always to clear up the mess left behind by men using the gift of free will no better than by advantage-taking and profit-grabbing, hurting others without wasting a thought on their miserable fate? Was it not men's own noble task to help the ones who stumbled in their tribulations, for truly to deserve their names as humans made to be the pride of creation?

Nature's laws can not be altered to fit everyone's needs differently for whatever an occasion. So it is up to men to help each other conquering life's hardship. Waiting for miracles is of no use since rules have to be straight and definite. One can not jump off the rooftop and expect a soft landing.

Similar, although sometimes less obvious, are consequences of deeds done. Inescapable as they are, sooner or later they will show. For what would happen to life without consequences? If pain was not to exist, people would live straight on without much thinking. A finger cut off by careless handling of tools – so what!, aren't there still nine others?

Pain and harm, as a warning before it is to late, are vital. Organs deteriorating by an overindulging lifestyle are likely to suffer a painful, yet highly educative, feedback one day. A world, heading to go up in flames, probably will see smouldering and fumes first, to attract due attention of its dwellers to do something about it and avert calamity. If not, they'd had it.

When meeting Jesus, the Commander-in-chief Cyrenius in late-night discussions asked about gnawing hunger, burning thirst or freezing frost – would men's strive for spirituality not be choked by it? He pleaded for elimination, or at least relief, of physical distress and poverty. After all, humans were spiritual beings, destined to achieve nobility of mind. But made of flesh and bone how could they when starving or freezing to death or perishing in wars?

Individuals under physical distress, struggling for survival, lacking the means to rise to the level of awareness of their immortal souls, – should not everybody's most fundamental physical needs be secured as a basis for spiritual progress?

Jesus did not doubt the noble motivation of the request but countered that mankind would not fare well by getting gratuitous delivery of every-day's demand without exerting due commitment themselves. Whole nations which by strike of luck had lived in abundance, finally adopted the habit of letting things deteriorate. In the end, they became so sluggish that they caused their own destruction.

Where have all the cities gone, the mighty ones? Where Babylonia, the Great, in days of old the centre of a world of splendour, glory and sinful pleasures? Dust drifted over the vast empty plains along River Euphrates, until thousands of years later the leftovers were dug out the soil beneath the debris of a forgotten past.

Hardship and worries were evolution's basic elements, causing mankind to become ingenious. Entrance free of charge to paradise, while living on Earth, was not provisioned. And the ones living on the sunny side of the world, were given ample opportunity to think of their less lucky brothers and sisters unless they wanted to share their very fate themselves one day.

What true humanity accounted for and what Jesus disputed with the ruler over half of Africa and

Asia, was that we are responsible for each other. Which hardly would be aware to us if everybody lived his life separately in well-being and splendid isolation, without the need of constantly to interact with fellow citizens. Cyrenius understood at least.

Further examples highlighted previous ones, bordering on indelicacy. Truth never being delicate anyway, Jesus compared life without hardship to a kraken sitting at the bottom of the sea, its tentacles gripping the luscious things, fish and other goodies, swimming around. It stuffs them into its belly until it almost bursts and that, bare of any further initiative, is the essence of its life.

Is that all? When abundance is unlimited, it tends to lead to idle laziness, everything beyond the most essential being forgotten „A bounty of blessed harvests, given by me for a hundred years in continuation, would result in mankind's horrendous slothfulness", was the Lord's final comment on the issue.

Labour and effort in the long struggle beneath the stars are necessary conditions of life – the failing and the showing of scars, and the glory won when fighting one's way to ever greater heights.

9. Mysteries of the Universe

Scientific facts like the existence of the solar system – today's knowledge of every little child – in ancient times only a few chosen ones had access to. But truth-seekers sensed that Jesus knew more about it. As if being called by an inner voice they were attracted from all directions to see him to have their questions answered.

Time and again the mystery of the universe was a main topic. Men like Roman administrators suspected Earth not to be a flat disc and that in far away civilisations of East-Asia its true nature was known. They asked Jesus for further enlightenment. Their wish being granted, he, out of thin air for better understanding, created the model of a miniature sun orbited by its planets.

What they saw made them gaze in amazement and confirmed their assumption. They espied the sun as the centre of a whirl of planets and other mysterious objects. Especially striking to them was the harmonic order of distances of the planets while orbiting. At a certain spot, however, an interruption showed. Where a planet was to be, was none!

Ages later, when astronomic sciences developed, it was noticed as well. By the invention of telescopes, within the sphere of the supposed but missing planet a myriad of small and smallest objects were detected, all of them circling the sun in different orbits. They were given the name of Asteroids.

Less than a century ago a common theory had them to be the debris of a broken-up planet, perished in space in a disaster for whatever a reason. Today the theory is largely abandoned in favour of the assumption that they are chunks of matter never reaching the state of forming a genuine planet. Strange thing though, they all are assembled within one zone, hundreds of thousands of them, whereas, given the huge expansion of the solar system, they could have spread equally all over the vast space. Why did they not? Was it an unpleasant truth, to be hidden some way or other?

There quite well would be a reason to shy away from a frightening fact if what was presented by Jesus would be taken seriously. It was about the gap in the solar system and, indeed, the object missing once had been a planet!

Ages back, this celestial object was to become the home of a human race to ascend to unprecedented heights above any other beings in the universe. The best of spiritual talents were granted to its dwellers, the gift of free will being the most crucial. As God's chosen children, they were supposed to reach ever higher levels of awareness, yet purely out of their own insight, never to be puppets on the strings of unknown forces.

The calamity of the planet might have begun with little violations of given divine laws, same as it had been a simple apple that triggered vexation on Earth. Small quarrels might have led to bigger ones, causing misdoings and treacheries. In the course of time, the free will became an obsession but it solely was the own will, not the one of others, that was seen. It was turned against any dissenter when not complying with the rules of those coming to power. The suppressed ones, naturally, had their own free will too, with the result that in the end mankind disintegrated into fractions fighting each other on life and death.

They devised the most evil weaponry. Jesus mentioned grain-like explosives, matter, processed by methods invented by super-brains with their vile intentions. The substance, if its energy was released, had the potential to be of a devastating power.

The end: Deep underground, the planet's inhabitants dug huge systems of tunnels stretching out to the territories of adversaries, from where they blasted them out of existence. What they did not know, or did not care to know, was the special characteristic of the matter they dug and mined into in ever further layers of the deep. The matter in the depth possessed the quality of self-ignition, a sort of chain-reaction that was not to be controlled once it started. Which exactly was what happened in an hapless hour of disaster and the planet exploded and was torn into a million pieces. Anxieties about the status of the earth we live on, would be pure speculations.

Or rather not? Some disclosures are found in

New Testament's Revelations of John if the language is understood, suggesting a final disaster that is looming. But among words of doom there are words of hope, that God will not allow the total annihilation of mankind again. The reference to the „multitude, clothed with white robes and palms in their hands" is the promise that Earth will be saved in times to come as the home of dwellers allowed to infinitely continue striving for spiritual truth.

The broken-up planet, many times bigger than Earth, had its debris scattered between the orbits of Jupiter and Mars, partly falling onto these planets, onto the earth and even the sun. But a great deal continued to orbit inside the sphere the former planet had occupied – an interesting challenge for future space missions? Since Moon long since was claimed to be travelled to, purportedly, and exploration of planet Mars on its way, Asteroids might prove to be the next worthwhile objects to examine. The Great Gospel of John foretells what to expect:

„The inhabitants, physically gigantic by size, were hurled into open space by the planet's bursting ... some sit or lie dead and totally mummified in their still existing houses on the bigger fractions of the debris ... "

The question arises, whether the planet's fate could have been diverted by warning the inhabitants? Yet, in further detailing, the records state: „The people hat been admonished and warned beforehand, again and again, for ages. They sternly were shown the results of their viciousness. Holding on to their worldly prudence, they simply shrugged it off, dismissing the predictions as unsubstantial phantasms, „... the great and noble ones did not only disbelieve them (the humble visionaries) but persecuted them in all directions with fire and sword ... everyone daring to raise concern, written or outspoken, mercilessly was killed ... in utmost cruelty".

As time went by, the mission to follow the perished planet in succession was assigned to Earth and its dwellers. To make it better. Will they ever do?

The solar system being explained and other visible planets as well, questions came up about further planets still undiscovered if there were any. Jesus affirmed their factual existence but due to immense distances they were not visible to the naked eye. Any details, he said, would be relevant only after the invention of technical means for their observation, in a far-away future.

This future finally had come in 19th century. General knowledge rapidly increasing, a technological upsurge set in with scientific breakthroughs widely celebrated. As for spiritual values, rather a marginal sense remained.

In 1842 – the seventh planet, Uranus, already being discovered by chance – Jakob Lorber, by his inner voice, received words of the existence of an eighth planet, given the name of Miron, that is World of Wonder. The ample account went beyond astronomical data only. Its territories were described, plants and the wildlife of animals and the social life of a mankind living there.

A celestial body, approximately a thousand times larger than Earth with a multiple distance to the sun, clearly displayed very different living-conditions for its human-like population.

Given the huge size of the planet, its individuals were very much bigger than their counterparts on Earth, yet physically of great beauty. Living in family clans in rural communities, they had little sense for technic and none at all for amassing riches. Their concern was to help each other and share possessions. General peacefulness prevailing, no governments and mass organisations evolved with all their laws and regulations.

Four years after Lorber disclosed the planet's existence, it was discovered by the outer world as well and was named Neptune. It was considered a great achievement of science although it solely appeared as a tiniest dot in the celestial spheres by observation of telescopes.

It took another hundred years till observatories and telescopes had the degree of perfection to disclose more of the planet's special conditions. Even if given credit to the possibility of extraterrestrial life in the universe, evaluations showed the planet's total uninhabitable nature, a cluster of eternal ice at the outmost fringe of the solar system in everlasting twilight, with temperatures of two hundred degrees Celsius below freezing point.

Had they, in their institutions, studied the given specifications about Miron/Neptune in detail, they might have found that their estimation was right but not entirely right: Explanations by Jesus, asked for by his followers, had it that the planet was surrounded by an atmosphere of vast dimensions, with a reflecting surface of immaculate purity at its outer fringe. It displayed the effect of an optical lens, to collect the sun's sparsely emitted rays of light and direct them to the equatorial region. Against the planet's size it might be considered a small area, but compared to terrestrial proportions it still was huge.

By the re-directed sunlight to this zone they had agreeable temperatures there for living conditions while the rest of the planet remained buried under its shield of ice. To adapt to their planet's sparsely incoming light, the inhabitant's eyes had developed specific structures, fully compensating for the deficit, permitting a perfect sight.

The strange phenomenons of Miron aroused the listener's quest for further revelations. They especially wanted to know about Moon and Sun.

The Moon: Orbiting its planet, it once rotated round its own axle, showing the full spectrum of its surface to would-be spectators on Earth. It possessed water and an atmosphere which always readily moved to its far side, due to the centrifugal force of its relatively swift circling, thus being undetectable by terrestrial observance. When the friction of the moving masses slowed down the rotation, it eventually came to a standstill and Moon showed itself from one side only. Air and water always remaining on the far side, they provided the basis for life of a primitive, yet human-like, civilisation.

The alternating shifts of extreme temperatures forced the populace to hide and stay below surface most of the time for cover against heat and frost. Between the monthly turning of day and night they had, for a short while though, a reasonable fair climate to grow various plants for nutrition.

The Sun: Due to presumed surface-temperatures of 5000 degree Celsius, the assumption of possible organic life is decried an absurdity by science. Quite contrary to it, revelations disclosed to Lorber speak of the existence of rich civilisations. Since circumstances are completely different, it is obvious that human life as known can not be sustained on Sun, a million times bigger than Earth. Life there must be in accord with its own physical condition.

Science's prevalent assumption is that Sun's energy derives from continuous thermonuclear fusion within itself. Disclosures revealed to Lorber being in total opposition thereto, explain that its light originates from radiation of the universe, mirrored by the surface of Sun's vast surrounding atmosphere. It reflects the light emanated by uncountable trillions of stars of the galaxy and spheres beyond, many of them celestial objects in magnitude dwarfing Sun unendingly. It is a radiation from ranges of space as vast and incomprehensible as infinity and eternity itself.

Human eyes are not made to percept this radiation. But on Sun, striking the surface of its surrounding atmosphere, it reflects as visible light, being the precondition of all life. The actual physical ground beneath is well protected from the vast energy above by an atmospheric shield, therefore not being accessible to observation. But it is said that they have ideal conditions of life there which enable the existence of many rich civilisations.

The inquisitive Romans and Greeks, as well as the simple minded disciples, ever again came up with more questions. They inquired about the overall extension of the universe itself. Jesus' frank answer was: You would not be able to understand! Nevertheless, he tried his best to bring forth a raw description to his listeners.

Our solar-system as part of the galaxy together with uncounted scores of other suns and their planets, is orbiting around a celestial centre many million times bigger than ours, a sun as well, yet visible only as a star among others due to the vast distance.

The time of one orbit's revolution being approximately 28000 years, it generates major shifts on Earth like changing meteorological conditions, the constantly varying climate, and alternating states of the oceans. Their waters accumulate on the southern hemisphere half of the time, as it is at present, then go to the northern side. In one hemisphere new landmasses with revitalized fertility of soil rise out of the floods, on the other side they sink below the oceans. Geologists probably have something to say when analysing sediments of different layers of the depth, the results of innumerable floodings, repeatedly occurring over the many millions of years.

The survey given to the listeners disclosed realms of the universe ever the greater in their extension. Our celestial region, with uncountable stars belonging to it, was said to be not more but a grain of dust in the endlessness of space when rotating itself around even a greater centre.

And so it went on: Further systems of super-suns rotated around other more gigantic ones, which in turn were part of celestial structures of inconceivable vastness – in trying to comprehend it blew the listener's mind, sending it spiralling.

Trying to grasp the essence of infinity ended in mental exhaustion. Ordinary folks like the disciples, as well as the men of science, despaired of their incapacity to understand. Further explanations were skipped. To advance to full understanding, men first were to become dwellers themselves of the unending world of eternity.

10.   Uniqueness of Earth

Once the high-commissioner Cyrenius proposed to Jesus they'd travel together to Rome, centre of civilisation, to introduce him to the high nobility. He was to guarantee that even the emperor, his uncle, would honour Jesus as the Messiah fulfilling his divine mission. All of the great empire's potential and facilities would be to his command to end wars and vileness, transforming Earth into something next to paradise.

Jesus did not misconceive the noble motivation of the proposal but his concern was not about paradise. Nor was it with power, which he unendingly commanded himself throughout the universe. The creation, though, of a world of free, self-determined beings never was to be achieved by decree; it was to be laboured for by men themselves. To help in the progress had been the reason for his incarnation, descending to Earth in humbleness as a newborn child, seeing the light of day in a mere stable.

Other worlds existed, inhabited by noble beings living in harmony and beauty which they had gotten as gifts without efforts of their own. But the knowledge of true divinity, and the option to strive for ever greater heights in life, was not theirs. Although, whenever a rumour about humans on planet Earth reached their worlds, they longed to be like them – and shied away the same time. Because choosing to follow them would have meant to renounce all of their own life's glory. Everything they had was to be left behind if ever they'd decide to be born as earthly humans, poor and miserable as it might turn out when forced to entirely live by themselves.

Not, that there was no glory and magnificence on Earth as well. But mainly it was where those in power dwelled, their mansions reaching up to the skies, built and maintained by labouring masses which sometimes hardly knew what to make a living from. To come to their relieve when aggrieved, Jesus had undertaken his mission, if only they were to recognize it and listen to his words.

For all the lectures about the universe, the one question remained: „O Lord, why is it that little Earth was chosen, tiny spot in unending space, you came to live on. Why is it unique, as you say, in the endless cosmic spheres? Weren't there worlds of much greater glory and beauty to your command?" His answer unveiled that Earth was unique indeed, but inquiring was one thing and understanding the complexity of the answer was another.

To critical minds the claim, Earth being the centre of all celestial worlds, borders on insanity. Less than a grain of dust at the edge of a galaxy which in turn hardly is more than a dot in the universe, it exists among countless other worlds in the intergalactic space. What made the difference to declare it unique?

In answering, Jesus compared the huge world of the universe to the small, but no less complex, world of the human organism, which is gifted with warm, pulsating life – why? Life's existence or absence easily is diagnosed but its essence, what it does consist of and why it is out of reach of men to create it themselves, is unknown. Scientists may analyse, experiment and manipulate to alter life's manifestations, but once it is gone only decay remains which no-one is able to prevent.

Life as created, exclusively granted out of spheres of divinity, is flowing into bodies through an organ of the tiniest quantity in relation to the overall organism. By physical means this organ's entity never is to be detected, as a soul never will be found by a scalpel in an operation. This particle of no dimensions, compared to the whole of the organism, is located inside the heart, the centre of existence and, in a way, God's own territory.

Essentially, people had known it right from the beginning of the creation. How else all the terms could have found their way into the languages, putting cordiality and heartiness in relation to the human heart, when something is hearty or heartwarming or done with a heavy heart. The heart can bleed or meld or be saddened and broken in heartrending heartbreak except when one has a heart of flint. A faint-heart can try, nonetheless, to take heart, not letting his heart sink into his boots. A heart can skip with joy, it can be lost to, or even stolen by, sweethearts and a great deal more, as everyone knows by heart.

To come to full circle: Without this tiniest organ inside the heart, men never would have been connected to life and consciousness. For it is essential in the constant exchange with spheres above, pulsating back and forth. Its tininess and uniqueness, compared to the whole of the body, is like the earth in comparison to the vast universe. And as a matter of fact, both can not exist without each other.

Through our very own planet unlimited cosmic energy is flowing in eternal progression. In return, what is lived through on Earth, the fighting and the loving, glory and greatness, failures and injuries, pain suffered and evil turned into blessing in the long struggle of the ages – it all is redistributed to the whole of the cosmos, in exchange for its gift of ever renewed life, urging men to constantly be on the move towards their divine destination.

„You would not yet understand", Jesus again said to his amazed listeners, „but once you have fulfilled your mission on Earth, you will."

Meanwhile, other areas of the human body largely being explored, the potential unfolded to substitute its various parts, either by artificial devices or by transplantation of living matter. The state is reached that nearly everything is replaceable, with the prospect of turning the body almost into a walking spare part-magazine. From the medical branches' point of view it probably is a desirable trend, their income heavily relies on it.

But what about the centre of life inside the heart? Will it also be substituted because dawn of heart-transplantation has broken, rendering all esoteric speculations to be absurdities?

In medical research centres human hearts must have been rated as spare-parts right from the beginning, else they would not have pushed so hard for appropriate technologies.

Yet, transplanting living hearts poses severe questions: What about the original owner, the donor? Overall consensus had it that he was dead and not in need to keep it for himself any longer. But unquestionably, he had to be alive enough in dying to secure future functioning of his heart, for a heart in decay is useless. So, when ex-planting it, everything to be done in a hurry, who is to guarantee that the donor is well and truly, absolutely dead?

Questioning the matter proves provocative. And how long would it be that, given the well-known shortage of hearts, donating sort of had to be encouraged? After all, big money is engaged.

It mustn't necessarily be handled in front of one's own doors, though. The world is big enough to look for fresh supplies elsewhere, being nobody's business then. A scenario, simple-hearted contemporaries might have no idea how far already it is a reality.

In addition, inquisitive minds ponder over how it feels having a spare heart, former centre of life of an other human. To prevent repulsion of physical tissue, incompatibly foreign to the receiver's body, a lifelong immune suppressing medication is mandatory. Which leads to the question of repulsion of still existing psychic leftovers, especially weird emotions of former owners, in case of mental incompatibility of donor and receiver? Inquisitive minds, digging deep enough, discovered some quite disturbing facts when they had a closer look at the matter.

But surely pharma industry, eager to correct God's imperfect creation, will come up with answers to the problem as well. Will they, really?

Travelling through the country together with the disciples, their master healed the sick and consoled the downtrodden. He freed prisoners perishing in gloomy dungeons. A faint whiff by him, a thought only, would have let the prison walls crumble to dust. But he obeyed the law, demanding the bail-out of the miserable. Burdened with guilt because of some misdemeanour committed, they had become captives unable to meet obligations to buy their way out. Shadows only of themselves, they were rotting towards the end of their lives.

Once Jesus paid their debt with money donated by a wealthy patroness. As a result, he was decried by the Templars of illegally wasting fortunes of others in phony pity on human write-offs. Regrettably, the whole of it would not be to their own disposal if ever they'd get a chance to grab it by juridical dodging, as they used to do in dealing with properties of single-living women and widows.

The travellers, accompanying Jesus, at times were many more than the Twelve, later-on known as the apostles. All of them were eager to contribute to their common cause but, consequently, they had to be catered for too when being on the move. Staying overnight somewhere, the comfort varied. Sometimes it were but simple cobblestones at the side of the road to lay their weary heads upon. Improved convenience though, was found at caravansary guest-houses along big trading routes where caravans, consisting of hundreds of men and animals, were on their way from Asian countries to markets at the Mediterranean Sea.

To proprietors, the catering for so many people required professional stockpiling, yet, supplies failing to come in, shortages had to be reckoned with. Ordinary food though, like bread and wine, was at hand anytime, being the disciples' first request when coming to a place. If, in addition, some well-prepared fish was available it was all they wished for.

At times though, fish were in short supply and the places' owner had to apologize for having none left in his ponds and water basins. It was no easy task to always get them fresh and alive from River Jordan or the Sea of Galilee with its richness of fish. Especially because transport in special tanks had to be fast to keep losses low.

One day, when saying 'sorry, no fish left', the

principal was encouraged by Jesus to have a second look. His ponds being emptied to the last meagre fishtail, he considered it useless but, displaying goodwill, he went to look. Afterwards he rubbed his eyes in astonishment, finding the ponds brimming over with fish. In what secret spots, for heavens sake, had they been hiding away? Immediately all hands of cooks and servants were set in motion and not before long an exquisite supper was readied for the just arrived guests.

The fish being of best varieties, lovely smell drifting all through the place, it was recognized at neighbouring tables where Pharisees happened to be seated. Used to premium service, they ungraciously complained and sent for the principal: Why was it they themselves were denied the delicacy? Known for their authoritative behaviour, they were not especially cherished as customers.

Everything ordered had been delivered!, was the answer they had to be satisfied with. Which did not please them, and their ill temper did not improve by overhearing the lively chatting at the other tables. Pharisees took it for granted to be the centre of all conversations, everybody paying due attention to them. Yet, nobody did. Besides, snapping up bits and pieces, the abominable feeling crept into their minds that the newcomers were sympathisers of the infamous conspirator of Nazareth.

For moderate use there was wine on their tables to loosen tongues and cherish minds. The Pharisees, malcontent as they were, felt obliged to loudly comment on the company of the disciples as soakers and boozers, accusing them of religious misconduct. No wonder, they sneered, given the sort of a leader they were running after! The last straws were insinuating remarks about women thought to be affiliated with the company. Enough was enough! The landlord, a Roman citizen, advised the scoffers to change rooms or take leave altogether.

When staying in townships, residents of the community were invited to the company's gatherings, often continued till late in night. Being open minded people, they were eager to listen and discuss what Jesus had to say about various issues of social life, the education of the young or the role of the sexes. His position was considerably different from what is propagated in today's widespread views.

Questions of political or economic significance were raised, or of health care and prevention of diseases. Cases of murder and robbery were looked at and how the villains be treated when caught. Death penalty widely being executed, Jesus not exactly was against lawful punishment but he saw the raging vengefulness of the offenders trying to wreak havoc on Earth after they were sent to the world beyond. If they, still living in their physical bodies, were possibly amended, it would be a turn for the better to everyone.

In the dead of night, listeners felt encouraged to pose further questions. Earth' mysterious uniqueness often was an issue again. Again comparisons were drawn to the tiniest organ of life inside the human heart, unknown to medical science, never to be detected by surgery.

Today it might be called a gateway, interfacing physical and spiritual worlds. All expressions of life owe their existence to this centre of no extent, without which, Jesus said, „all limbs be dead and immovable, the way idols of brass are". The energy from spheres of eternity was to flow through it to regions of common life, a constant taking and giving back and never a standstill which would have meant death. Life, generated in regions of countless stars, was passed on to Earth while the essence of everything endured and lived through by humankind was interwoven in what was to be returned to the ranges of the universe.

Few fully comprehended the matter but those who truly understood, Jesus called „my friends and brothers", to stay with him forever, his words coming to life in their hearts.

Resting after their late conversations, Jesus preferred to spent the night in a comfortable armchair, as they were in use at the dining tables. Asked why, he stated that half upright a position would be more natural concerning blood circulation than sleeping stretched out horizontally.

11. Betrayal in Pre-stage

In dealing with contemporaries, Jesus was of almost unending patience. If misguided, heading to wrong directions, he let them have their will knowing they as immortal souls had to return be it even after ages of time in another form of existence.

A most outstanding example of divine patience is revealed by the fate of Judas Iscariot, the betrayer. Why did Jesus accept him as a disciple in the first place? Was he not to foresee the resulting disaster?

The question is partly to be answered by a counter-question: Would it have been for the world's benefit if Jesus had warded off all offences in superiority and, after finishing his task on Earth, comfortably retired and peacefully died in bed? Judas very well had to play his role in the ongoing events.

As it was, the other disciples fiercely would have liked to send him to remote wastelands never to come back. They considered him weird, a jack of all trades but a master of none. They wondered when Jesus finally was to lose his temper. Reasons were more than enough but Judas always was pardoned and so he stayed on.

Compared to the other disciples' characters, shaped by their humble social background, Judas was of sophisticated appearance he had acquired when practising various professions in different places. As a self-declared expert in financial transactions, he at times was of bustling activity and offered to take over administration and exchequer of their missionary movement.

Yet now and then, he did not mind a sip of wine, or more, and consequently was left behind when sleeping off his drunkenness while the others were on their way to new missions. Until he eventually caught up with them. But sometimes he was absent for longer periods, engaged in cryptic activities of his own. The disciples hoped for the day he would stay away for good but were disappointed. Judas was not to get rid of.

It all began when Thomas, one of the disciples, left the community for a short visit to where his family was living, rendering enthusiastic accounts to the village folk of what he was engaged in. Among the listeners had been Judas who at once sensed the chance to hook up with a world of magical power he deemed to profit from.

At that time, he had been in a fix, miserably making a living by trading pottery. As the only son of a well-to-do family he had seen better days but all the wealth had melted away in dubious transactions and a ruinous lifestyle.

Convinced to have learned from his blunders, he hoped for a streak of luck when joining the fellowship of the disciples. He offered to contribute his know-how in matters of finance but it fell short of his expectations: Jesus called monetary profit the

„excrement of hell", save it be used for deeds of charity. To Judas, driven by his craving for wealth and influence, it was quite sobering but did not put him off.

He never understood what Jesus was to bring to the world. Amazing miracles happened in his presence, yet Judas interpreted them as the tricks of a great magician. Hoping for schooling and instruction, he was eager to achieve similar abilities leading to riches and power. Money and prestige being big issues in his life, he well was in lockstep with general values treasured throughout society.

To his conviction, money being the only way to effectively handle the world, Jesus replied that unswerving trust in God would be worth more than any treasuries imagined. Judas' response was that the emperor himself had authorised the utilisation of money in his empire to facilitate trading among the citizens. So, it was for the benefit of everyone and its use possibly no sin? Besides, it kindly could be given to the poor for relief.

Embarrassingly, Jesus reminded him that it was he himself habitually passing by beggars without ever opening his purse. And of the fact that it had been Satan who invented money for potential sinners to be tempted by its easy use.

As an example, the thriving prostitution in the cities was pointed to, where the owners of pieces of gold were encouraged to sin day and night whatever their nature allowed. In ancient times of barter trading sheep, chicken or field crops, business would have been much more complicated.

Dark times of his life being touched, Judas listened to Jesus' rebuke with a sour face. But he was not discouraged, nor did he cease to praise the advantages of financial management, until he was given a prophetic forecast: „In not too far away a future you will find out the curse of money all for yourself".

At times, the disciples were extremely upset about their mate Judas. To them, he not only showed a somewhat lessened respect towards their master but they considered him a nickel nurser despite his brilliant financial theories. And, they caught him red-handed when exploiting the gift of healing, granted to them by Jesus at a special occasion.

They had been sent to surrounding villages to self-reliantly heal the sick, after stern admonition never to charge any fee from the ailing. Yet, Judas managed to return from his missions with his pockets filled, declaring their content as „voluntary gifts of gratitude". When criticised by his colleagues, as by Thomas, he brazenly paid him out in his own coin. One word followed the other, things were escalating and a hefty scuffle was under way.

Thomas, boiling with rage, was short of using his fists when Jesus stepped in and intervened, saying: "Brother, as long as you see me staying calm and easygoing you stay easy as well. Solely, if you do see me punching, come and join the fight. But for the rest, let Judas be Judas as we are what we are. I did not invite him, so I do not send him away. Will he go all by himself we do not weep. But you stay away and forgive him, as I forgive him, and your mind will be at ease".

Sometimes Judas vanished, being away in own affairs until he reappeared, bragging about his achievements in pursuing their common cause. Which, by all means, was quite a reality for he was intelligent and a brilliant speaker in public who attracted his audience. Contrary to most of the others, he was skilled in writing and reading and he knew how to support his positions by appropriate quotations of the scriptures' old prophets.

Places he visited became the scenes of campaigning for Jesus. People, which previously had heard all sort of rumours, showed up in droves for curiosities sake when he held a speech. Besides, he engaged himself in fund-raising for their common cause, securing a modest share to his own pockets for expenses. He meant to foresee a great future of their movement and did not deem it wrong to pay attention to questions of financing, regardless of what others said.

Sometimes, however, he was carried away by fantasies so much he ended up ranting until Jesus bluntly told him: „You lie!" Which had a sobering effect for a while to have him exercising care in what he was saying.

Once, Judas being absent, Jesus gave an explanation to the disciples why their mate had turned out to be the man he was, overseeing everything right from the beginning of his life.

Judas was the only offspring of wealthy parents. Father and mother were attached like mad to their little golden boy, mollycoddling him wherever they could. They gave him everything he had a craving for, no matter how insane it was. Developing all sorts of bad habits, they let him get away with them.

They let the sapling grow the way it did and, by their education, they had the sprouting plant ever the more crooked. When the trunk was grown and hardened there was not much to be done afterwards to straighten it out. A soul, once it was twisted, hardly ever turned out to be an upright character.

The result? As a talented young man, on his way to masculinity, he stormily engaged in orgies of passion with the ladies offering their services, testing the limits of his virility. Thus he wasted the hard-worked-for fortune of his elders and betters, turning them into beggars, dying prematurely of grieve and sorrow. Judas, a have-not by then, was called in public a scoundrel and wretch. Which at long last, as he had to admit to himself, was a sad reality.

But it was too late for self-reproach and he eased himself by imagining the root of the evil must have been with his parents' education: Why did they fail to raise him properly? He impossibly could have educated himself, so, he concluded, the deterioration of his life as it was could not have been his own fault.

But how to continue? He found himself completely broke with not even a place of shelter left. He considered a criminal career but quickly abstained from the idea. Draconian punishment was exerted in public and watching executions terrified him. So he swallowed the bitter pill of engaging in a trade, pottery. Poorly done as his products were, he sold them in marketplaces, just about barely to make a living.

And yes, he started a family. But wife and children got to know him from quite a different angle. As generous he had been to the ladies of his former life, as tight-fisted and harsh he proved to be to his own kin, and what he did to them better should be covered under blankets of silence. He was obsessed with visions of getting rich while his family was living in bitter poverty.

When joining Jesus he was not really interested in religious findings but rather in methods to effectuate miracles to get hold of big and fast money. It was to be foreseen that he steered a course towards disaster.

Money, when used sensibly, had its value insofar as it is an agent of life in social spheres if allowed to move. Like blood in the body, money must circulate, otherwise it coagulates, turning into clots, blocking essential functions. They call it 'infarct': On one side too much, on the other nothing. As cells die in a living organism when choked, congestion occurs in social life when a few own close to everything and the rest barely nothing.

Strangled by regulations to fit the interests of rulers, communities deteriorate when denied exchange and circulation of what people were to give to each other, products and skills, thoughts and visions. There was no objection to a modest use of money as long as it supported these goals of vital communities' development.

But Jesus foresaw that the church he founded when choosing disciples, would not lead to gentleness and charity alone. Once being big enough, the movement would be taken over by forces claiming religious authority, yet corrupt it from within by amassing riches for secular glory, waging wars and ruling the world by their financial system.

The true church, however, was meant to be erected without sacral buildings, ceremonial vestment and worldly power. The riches, sought for by men, existed inwardly only, in loving hearts.

The Bible tells about Jesus' mission on Earth the way it began: „Jesus was led by the Spirit into the wilderness to be tempted of the devil ... he taketh him up to an exceeding high mountain and sheweth him all the kingdoms of the world and their glory ... and saith unto him, All these things will I give thee if thou wilt fall down and worship me". Behold! Worship the Lord of Mammon! The answer had been: „Get thee hence, Satan, for it is written Thou shalt worship the Lord thy God, only". An answer never to forfeit it's validity up to the present day.

12. Women

Reports mention Jesus' and his disciples' gratefulness when invited to an hospitable home after a
long day of dusty roads, and offered a sound and
proper meal. It were the women in the background
catering for the guests and creating an atmosphere
of hospitality, gestures of kindness since time began.
Their service easily taken for granted, they, guardians of the family, cared for life in society and
passed it on through the generations.

An encounter, known from the bible, was at the well
in Samaria. The company had been on road all day,
the disciples being worn out and thirsty. Some lay
on the grass while others went to the nearby town
of Sichar to buy food. Jesus, weary and thirsty too,
sat down at the edge of the well but there neither
was a bucket nor a rope to draw water and the well
was deep.

A woman came with a pitcher, sank it below the
surface by a long cord and drew it up without taking notice of the waiting stranger. But Jesus addressed her, saying: „Woman, I am thirsty, give me to
drink." Noticing the way the man was dressed, the
woman identified him as a foreigner of a tribe
unfriendly to her own kin. She refused the plea. But

Jesus said: „You are blind! If you could see who I am you gladly would give. If you only knew what I could give you in return!"

The woman, though poor, judged by her worn outfit, was young and very beautiful. But she was proud too. She was used to male's lecherous looks at her and she mistook him for one of them. Her answer was snappish: Never should he dare to think she'd be at his will! He, who otherwise only would despise her!

Jesus did not lose his patience. What he had spoken of and was ready to give was the living water of his word that not only satisfied thirst but promised abundant life forever.

The woman grew uneasy, but what really made her confused was when Jesus began to tell about incidents of her life he as a stranger never could have known: Fife husbands, she successively had been married to, died one after the other, each within a year. The people of the town thought her body infested by some strange disease, killing everyone closely engaged to her. In the end, she believed it herself and vowed not to marry again. Never really feeling well, she feared the disease one day might be her own doom, too.

The woman, Irhael by the name, was shaken to the core, wondering who it was she talked to. She answered, not without some effort: „Sir, I see you must be a prophet. Since you know all of my life, you may know what might heal me?"

Fearing to have a sinful heart, she felt unworthy

in the stranger's presence. But Jesus said that it solely was her very heart he had the encounter arranged for with her. She well was known to him since the beginning of her life.

She did not in the least remember where they possibly could have met before, he entirely being a stranger to her. She more and more grew bewildered but was kindly asked if she ever forgot the childhood's incident of hers when she fell into a deep well and almost drowned in the water? It had been his hand that saved her and drew her out. And so he often had kept watch over her. Irhael sensed that the one she was talking to must be more than a mere prophet.

When, in their conversation, they touched the issue of the coming Messiah the world was waiting for, the woman eagerly asked to learn more about it. Could the Messiah be found and was he to help her if she beseechingly begged him with all her fervour? Jesus answered: „I that speak unto thee, am he!" Then he said: „Be healed!" And she was.

Realizing that something marvellous was happening inside her, Irhael was weeping with joy. She hurried to the nearby town, excitedly telling everyone about her strange encounter and what it did to her. The citizens hardly were to believe it, at first suspecting the ailing woman under a spell for some weird sins committed.

Yet, it caused quite a stir. The rumour all over the country of a newly arisen prophet – could it be that there was some truth in it and her story was credible anyway? To look for themselves, the crowd started out to see the one Irhael claimed to be the Messiah.

Meanwhile the disciples returned from town with bread, urging Jesus to eat. But he answered that he found something better than simple food: Hearts and minds craving for spiritual truth! When the host of the citizens arrived, sensing reality in what Irhael had spoken, they wanted to know more about it and the disciples soon found themselves engaged in explaining and interpreting their master's teachings to the many newcomers.

The people begged Jesus to stay on and he promised to be with them for two more days. A little argument did arise about whom be allowed to invite him. It was Irhael's invitation, given out of a heart overflowing with love, that was accepted.

Her place once had been an ancient castle, by grace of the municipality granted to her to live in. Spacious though, it hardly was more than a mere ruin but she promised to do everything at her command to satisfy the guests.

Jesus proposed to invite whoever had a desire to come, promising to look himself for the necessary arrangements. So all of a sudden servants arrived to take care of the preparations. An adolescent of stunning beauty showed up among them and lent a hand wherever it was needed, giving instructions and advice. No-one really knew how, but things successively turned out to be perfect, rotten structures of the building mysteriously improved and precious furnishing was found in hidden places to be brought to the rooms. Tables were set with all sorts of delicacies and dispositions were made to host a great number of guests.

To the citizens it was a grand event when Jesus and his companions stayed right on amidst them, answering the many questions they had, showing the way to alter their lives for the better. It was a great gift to them but the greatest gift was granted to Irhael.

Her dearest desire was to live with the man she secretly loved, a medic she once beseechingly had begged to help her. Healing being beyond his skill, he nevertheless had agreed to stay near her to ease her through the agony of her illness. He was stunned by her beauty but, being well aware of the danger, never dared to court her. Having known his integrity and his pure heart in the past, it was him Irhael wished to share her life with, more than anything in the world.

The threat of the disease lifted and no more contagion to be feared, Jesus united them both in orderly marriage.

A woman, also known from the scripture, is the adulteress. Adultery was considered an unforgivable sin, to be punished by death, often without circumstances taken into account. To poor young socially inferior females, physical beauty was a bitter burden when falling prey to the pursuit of rich males.

The young married woman the Bible mentions was caught in the very act. Instead of being stoned to death though, as demanded by law, she cunningly was dragged to the temple where Jesus was lecturing a host of people. He was asked: „What sayest thou?".

The pharisees, conducting the arrest, hoped to unmask him in front of the crowd as a law-breaker, who disobeyed the strict law given by Moses should he acquit the woman of her guilt out of pure mercy. Laws of Moses equalled the laws of God himself, so any feelings of sentiment were in a wrong place.

The following is quoted from the bible: „Jesus stooped down, and with his fingers wrote on the ground, as though he heard them not. So when they continued asking him, he lifted up himself, and said unto them, he that is without sin among you, let him first cast a stone at her. And again he stooped down, and wrote on the ground. And they which heard it, being convicted by their own conscience, went out one by one ... "

When Jesus looked up again, seeing the woman standing alone, he asked where her accusers went to and whether no-one had condemned her. She said: „No man, Lord." And Jesus said to her: „Neither do I condemn thee, go, and sin no more."

In the Great Gospel of John, a detailed supplement goes with it: The young woman never had in mind to sin, had it not been for dire need and the worry about her starving family. A Pharisee, dressed as a Roman nobleman, had pursued her with persuasive sweet-talk but ill intentions, promising generous gifts until he had her where he wanted her to be. The villain, however, had brought along the thugs of the temple-guards which brutally tore the unfortunate from the scene after the accomplished act, dragging her away without mercy.

To the people in the temple listening to Jesus, the incident's real cause was revealed by someone who knew the facts and bravely stood up to tell the truth. In the uproar that followed the villain made a narrow escape only and the thought of the infuriated crowd ready to lynch him might have sent him shivers down the spine as long as he lived.

Yet, there must have been a substantial number of unreported cases of similar crimes. Young women of the lowest class again and again were subject to pursuits, often after their and their families' existence perfidiously had been ruined, their sources of income disrupted, until they fell prey to the evil will of their pursuers. Caught afterwards, by priestly grace they were spared the stoning but, instead, disappeared behind the temple's walls into secret brothels as their fresh supplies. May the villains be crushed by divine wrath, was the public's general opinion about it.

Though Roman authorities tried to eliminate outright inhumanity by appropriate laws, slavery and its unjustness still was widespread. Male slaves usually were condemned to join the labour force whereas abominable reports of traded young women were heard of, helplessly being at their wicked owner's will. On the other hand, it was quite common that women were treated decently, even integrated into existing social structures. Polygamy being conventional, it was not unusual, when cooperating, that they were accepted as secondary wives in big tribal families. This widely was the custom in the prevalent Greek civilisations of the east.

Constantly being on the move, Jesus went to those places as well to deliver his message. Asked about true conditions of social life, his answers were distinct: Mankind was made as men and women, mentally and physically, to complement one another and live together as one couple for all of the lifespan. Only if circumstances had led to polygamy, it was to be continued in kindness. For a wife, when outcast, was bound to live in misery, with hardly any decent way to exist outside family structures.

There were no objections to buy slaves if they were treated well, given an education and eventually generously be freed. But selling them like merchandise was an act of abhorrence forever.

Religious life in countries outside Palestine still was marked by the belief in old pagan gods though hardly any faith was left in them. The priests continued ceremonies for convenience sake only but the thing was rotten to the core and just a kick would let it crumble. To Jesus, it was a reason to go there to visit them as well.

Travelling east to hamlets of River Euphrates, he came to a place where the local priesthood boastfully offered, for a modest charge, predictions of the future plus useful tips for every-day's needs, given by their gods Jupiter, Apollo and Minerva. Larger than life, they were sitting next to the wall of their temple, looking like being made of stone when off-duty. But they were said just to be waiting silently until invoked to life.

Jesus waved it off, the effort well to be spared. Rather the speakers, hidden behind the idols, were to set free to the light of the dear sun. But the big-mouthed priests severely warned him not to insult the gods by loose talk unless he was to evoke disaster. Everything was genuine they insisted. No speakers at all!

Jesus forgave them their impertinent lies but let the colossi disintegrate into thin air, all to crumble and vanish without a trace in one moment. Out crawled the speakers, flabbergasted and startled, from the now open narrow hollows behind.

The priests were confused as well when forced to acknowledge their profitable idolatry business had come to an end. Jesus advised them to take off their silly ceremonial vestment and look for another job. Still being bedazzled, they got the message.

Not so their wives, guardians of tradition and keepers of long-standing established values. When recognizing the enormous damage done, they were lost in misery: Not the slightest sign of the former divine glory left in the temple! Although they, too, did not believe in it any more but it had been the structural component of their community's social life where they, as spouses of the priests, were holding leading positions.

How to carry on when ordinary folk was to discover everything had been a deception? That rich gifts meant to appease angry gods were re-directed to the clergy's own pockets? People would grow rebellious, talks of revolution popping up, law and order falling apart, and earnings pouring to them so conveniently be gone with the wind. An impossible situation!

The women did raise a storm to have their priest-husbands to protest the unwelcome alteration in dead earnest and press for the restitution of the well-proven regime of old. Annoyingly, though, the men dissented and instead of listening they left to seek the company of the intruder.

By the end of the day, while the priests together with officials and respected citizens of the community met in a hall to listen to teachings of Jesus, the women decided to get something done of their own and, to that avail, had started to prepare the holy district of the temple's grove.

Next morning in early twilight when their husbands, a bit worn out, returned from the conference and passed the grove, they were struck by horrendous screaming and whimpering, menacing bawling and bellowing of coarse voices, interrupted by piercing shrieks. Bloody revenge it was the abandoned gods were swearing, cursing their unfaithful servants for breaching their vows. Frightened to the core, the men ran home.

While recovering from the terrifying shock, their wives rushed to the site of the grove to relieve the hired personnel, workers and maiden, from doing the trickery and detach the shrieking cats, tied by their tails. But all in vain! Someone must have laid a terrific spell on them. The domestics, hidden in the trees, were like glued to the branches with no way whatsoever to bring them down while the cats in the brushwood were biting and scratching so ferociously nobody dared to come near.

Back at the priests' domicile, Jesus showed up and explained the situation, not failing to mention that they themselves were accountable for the stubborn behaviour of their wives. The beautiful and greatly admired daughters of a high-priest they once had been in the prime of their lives, courted by their husbands-to-be, definitely could have done better. But being impressed by the religious deceit and witchcraft of their men, the women finally turned out to be close allies to perform the tricks and alleged miracles produced in the temple.

Not much to argue against, the priests ruefully accepted the blame and set out to look for the missing wives which despairingly, but still in vain, tried to release the paid wailers in the grove and free the furious cats. When the women spotted Jesus they begged him for forgiveness and the rescue of the servants. Which was granted at once, the captives easily climbing down from their hide.

The supernatural power of Jesus, whom at first they deemed to be a mere magician, could no longer be ignored; facts had to be accepted. Yet, it caused a mental conflict. Not only had the women abandoned their faith in old gods and goddesses but had scrapped any belief in a world beyond as well. Instead, they had taken to modern Greek philosophers like Diogenes who lived in a barrel, mocking human existence as an unsubstantial illusion which made him world-famous. On top of it, they had it mingled with elements of Indian esotericism, resulting in a blend fitting everybody's agenda.

Battling with words, the women tried to sustain their positions in upcoming discussions. Jesus had a hard time with their sharp tongues, especially when they widely amplified their thesis, talks of life after death being pure nonsense. Discussions wore on, heating up more and more, until the opponents were entangled in contradictions of their own distorted conceptions so much, that they were forced to acknowledge the wrong course they were steering. Finally, they too were ready to accept the new message that was brought to them.

Among the females, one must not be forgotten: Jarah, a tender maiden still, almost a child, inflamed in innocent love for Jesus, right from the beginning when she saw him.

She first attracted attention when Jesus, and a crowd following him, went along the shore of the Sea of Galilee. Displaying superiority over nature, he stepped onto the surface of the water, took a stroll out on the lake and called for others to come as well. Embarrassing silence. No-one had the guts to join, not even a military commander, accompanying the party.

No-one except Jarah. When Jesus called her she trustfully came skipping towards him, lively and brisk. Overcoming their fear, the left-behind gradually followed, even when by wind and upcoming waves the surface under their feet rather began to sway. Dancing and bouncing on the water, they had an unforgettable day, everybody finally joining the jolly crowd, even the commander.

Once intimacy was installed, it made Jarah and her sisters wish to stay with the company of the men in their father's big guest-house Jesus and the disciples were accommodated. But the father sent them off to inner rooms because little girls mustn't necessarily gawk at his guests nor stress their ears with fabulous gossip and small-talk.

Jesus praised his concern for the children's proper education but did not feel molested at all by the young folk – couldn't they come back, please? They could, thanks to divine intervention, and Jarah, the youngest, immediately ran up to her saviour, hugging him as if never again to let him go.

Her father grumbled at the intimacy, things going too far, he said, but Jesus replied that those rushing to him with such passionate love, the purity of heaven mirroring in their innocent souls, were the ones finding the path to God.

In the course of time, Jarah was given into Angel Raphael's custody who took her to spheres no living being ever had been to. With unfathomable wisdom she did return. Venerable, dignified old men, when meeting her, were aghast about what she had to tell. In their days of age, they had to accept that there still were many things to be learned they never had dreamed of.

Striving for wisdom all through their lives, they were at their wits' end when listening to this little girl. But no wonder, they said, she simply was getting everything for free by her heavenly protector and counsellor, Angel Raphael!

„Oh, him!", she cried, „never! If he gets a hint by the Lord, then yes, but for the rest he doesn't do anything. It's true, he is always kind and friendly, but just try to ask for more! 'You'll find out yourself', is all you get out of him!", she complained.

At an occasion, Angel Raphael being around in physical appearance, they straight-away asked him about it. He answered he only was to act according to the request of his Lord, be it a trifle or the creation of a whole world. If there was none, he would not do anything by his own. Yes, he was ordered to be her mentor, but even amiable young girls mustn't be coddled and spared own efforts.

Angel Rafael compared his power to that of big parabolic reflectors invented in Egypt. Being several arm's length in diameter, they deflected the incoming light of the sun towards a little point, the focus, concentrating its energy so much that everything getting close burst into flames the same moment and burned to ashes.

Similar was the sort of energy he drew from the Lord when assigned to a mission. When the task was accomplished, the energy would be null and void. Like the energy of a parabolic reflector is null and void, simply non-existent, once the sun is covered by clouds and not shining any longer.

13. Twin Sisters in Spirit

For ages, the character of famous Mary Magdalene was surrounded by legends. Was she a whore or was she a saint? Public opinion had it that immaculacy of morals was not her primary concern.

As sole heiress of rich parents, fondled by fortune, she inherited the family's palace and ample real estate. Being young and being a beauty, she successfully warded off intrusive suitors, preserved existent riches and added new ones. She was independent, intelligent and considered to be a great sinner, qualities which earned her quite a degree of fame. No small fraction of her clientele consisted of rich Pharisees.

Yet, despite living in sin, out of charity she took pity especially on the poorest of the poor. For the services offered she charged adequate fees to give them away to the ones living in bitter poverty and dire need.

Her activities, though, did not pass her by without leaving traces. Engaged with customers, she got infested with their ill demons which took possession of her whenever she was entrapped to drink wine. As a result, she was attacked by them in states of obsession she was not able to control, frightening casual bystanders by her weird reactions.

There again, she could charm people by manners of modesty when, as a hostess, she showed travelling strangers around to find their way in Jerusalem's big and bewildering city. As she did with a delegation of high ranking Romans whose arrival happened to be during a season of religious celebrations. The whole place being crammed with visitors, suitable accommodation nowhere was to be found, save by professional help which she was willing to provide.

Magdalene led the group of thirty men to a large guest-house some way outside the city, a division of the Lazarus properties. To the Templars it was ill-famed, out of the sole reason they did not possess it themselves which they had tried but failed to get hold of. Despite their constant defamation in public, it was a place of noble hospitality rarely to be seen elsewhere. By chance, Jesus and his disciples stayed there, too, unknown to outsiders.

Upon arrival, the Romans ordered a hearty meal which by its richness fully compensated for suffered hunger and thirst of a long and tiresome day. While eating and drinking, spirits lifted in merry criss-cross chatting about strange and funny things, a good deal of it being contributed by their pretty, and already rather hilarious, guide. The disciples, seated unrecognised at a distant table, eagerly listened to the affairs of a lustrous world they never even had known it existed.

The way things evolved had been a pleasant surprise to everyone. But then conversation took a turn to more serious subjects when the main speaker of the group reminded them of the real intention why they had ventured on the long and strenuous journey from far-away Rome right to this place: Was there any truth in the rumour of a newly-arisen prophet, performing most amazing miracles, healing and all? Back home in Rome, all sorts of myth had circulated when news had reached their city. The question in particular was posed to Mary Magdalene.

She did not know. Not that she hadn't heard of it but fabulous things always were said about prophets. Whether they added up to something real was another story. Rather not, was her belief, she never was to give special credit to prophets anyway, boring and gloomy as they were in her opinion like, as she said, a „cold and misty day in late autumn". But that only were her private views she was to press not on others. The leader of the Romans benevolently forgave his pretty companion for her somewhat loose talk and deemed it typical of her still juvenile giddiness.

In the course of the evening, for more substantial information, he contacted the landlord of the guest-house who, after a secret wink from Jesus, present but still unrecognized, shrugged off the request. It was not the right time yet.

But the very moment soon was to come. During the meal a significant amount of the excellent wine was consumed and finally, when a cup of it found its way into Magdalene's fingers, things happened which were bound to happen: She was seized by tremendous spasms, began to scream pitiably and her face, limps and muscles were twisted and distorted in such a terrible way the horrified guests were left to think the last hour of their guide, squirming in agony, had broken. Was it punishment of their pagan gods, a payback for being unfaithful to them when looking for others? What was to do?

Nothing, just wait, the hostel's principal said, the woman was known for the sort of reactions happening to her. And obscure pagan gods had nothing to do with it either, pure creatures of fantasy as they were, totally non-existent. As for help, there only was one who was able to.

This one was Jesus. He spontaneously stepped up and held his hands over the obsessed, threatening the evil demons possessing her to leave at once – and the woman got up safe and sound as if she never had been in troubles. Yet, she felt like being awoken from a strange dream.

Gazing at the man standing in front of her, her mind was bewildered, befallen by sudden remembrance: It was him! The same one! The only one! Times ago, she had but seen him passing by on the street, never again to forget the chance encounter till the end of her days, the eyes which had looked at her. Ever since, she had loved the unknown stranger with all the fervour of her heart.

The re-encounter brought it all back to her, but with no hope of her love ever being returned. Because she deemed herself a despicable whore – and him a nobleman of unreachable immaculacy.

The Great Gospel of John quotes Jesus' recount of what happened shortly after: „Hereupon she fell down on her knees, embraced my feet, and moistened them with tears of love and ruefulness."

The disciples, considering her behaviour abnormal, if not indecent, tried to drag her away. Jesus commanded them not to. Even if the woman had been sinning a great deal, what she was doing was done out of love for him. And he said to her: „Your sins are forgiven. But sin no more lest you be befallen by even worse harm!" In one single moment she was well and her character completely changed. All her future life's sole desire was to be near her saviour.

For several days Jesus stayed with the company of the inquisitive Romans, answering all their questions about conditions and regulations of life. They gained spiritual insights never found in Rome, centre of world's sciences, and got more than they ever dared to hope for.

Their gratefulness for this grand gift they extended to Mary Magdalene, who had been the intermediary for their encounter. But she thought herself an instrument only of divine intervention, unknowingly following a call to meet Jesus. Becoming fully aware of the all-embracing grace bestowed upon her, she again in thankfulness knelt down to his feet, washing them with overflowing tears and drying them with the richness of her hair.

Again, the disciples were annoyed by her behaviour but Jesus warded them off and said: „ All the time you have been with me, not one of you ever had shown his love for me so passionately".

Lazarus, who was unmarried, lived with his two sisters, Martha and Mary. After the healing and conversion of Mary Magdalene, a deeply felt friendship between the two sisters and her evolved, leading to the invitation to stay at their premises for good. In later days it was the reason for identities mixed up of the two Marys.

Mary, sister of Lazarus, belonged to the wealthy nobility and equally was viewed as a great beauty which made her the target of intrusive suitors, especially Pharisees. Making their advances, they definitely were not the best social contacts to her but she was not without blame. Fond of merrymaking, able to afford all sorts of amusement by her riches, she had earned a reputation of fun-loving which stuck to her.

When she got to know Jesus closer during one of his visits to Lazarus, when staying at their place as a guest, it completely changed. Sensing his divinity altered all of her life as it did with the other Mary, yet without mingling affections of her pure heart. Rejected suitors however, with their loose tongues, insinuated and blazoned forth in public Jesus as her favourite lover. But all the gossip was nothing but evil defamation. Living up to innocent love of Jesus became the sole motivation in her life.

Contrary to her, her sister in spirit Mary Magdalene still was entangled in feelings of ardent longing. The events afterwards, leading to the fulfilment of Jesus' mission by his crucifixion, must have been a heart-rending agony to her.

In the early light of Easter morning, blinded by tears in immeasurable grief, it was Mary Magdalene, being the first to hurry to the grave. When she met the Resurrected, whom at first she deemed to be the gardener before truly recognizing him, she fell down to his feet. But she was held back by the words: „Touch me not!" Drawing nearer to him, the passionate love would have been too much for her. Touching him would have cost her life.

Yet, she was the first to annunciate, to the disciples and hence to all of mankind, that a new era began by the Resurrection of Christ. Though the particulars of her fate got lost in the mist of legends, it can be assumed that, in the course of time, she was to adjust her feelings when, by spreading fame, she learned about the true divine nature of the one she loved dearest.

Finally, another Mary must be mentioned: „Mary, Mother of God". Jesus called her the 'bearer of my body'. Up to the last day, her life's sole concern was her son, enduring aching pain when, again and again for long periods of time, he had to leave her alone. She never ceased to warn him of the dangers when he exposed himself to the hazards of the outside world where blind men in their ingratitude tried to inflict harm on him. They never recognized that in reality he wanted to be none but the true saviour of theirs.

The dangers he had to conquer tore Mary's heart apart, and yet, in the end, it was she who stood, together with the women of her kin, near him under the gallows, the wooden cross he finally was nailed upon. Except for John, all the disciples had fled the scene in horror and panic.

Jesus foresaw a time when general adoration made Mary the Queen of Heaven whom more churches were dedicated to than to himself. But at Angel Gabriel's annunciation she had answered: „Behold, (I am) the handmaid of the Lord; be it unto me according to thy word." In unending humbleness she never wished to be more than God's servant. Jesus loved his mother dearly, but she, as part of the creation, was a human woman as well as others. This not to be forgotten, was his concern to transmit to the ages to come.

14. Shocking Events at Bethany

The chronicle of Jesus' life on Earth, transmitted by the inner voice from 1851 onwards, came to an end in 1864 when Jakob Lorber died, after a life in utmost modesty. Decades passed before a successor, beckoned to be a god-chosen scribe as well, continued the messages of the Great Gospel of John. Due to his different mental background, his work varies in phrasing but the recordings of Jesus' last days on Earth are as genuine.

They cover last journeys with the disciples when cordially being invited by the humble rural populace. Furthermore the events unfolding in Bethany and the retreat to a remote place for contemplation. It was followed by what happened at Holy Week in Jerusalem, of which detailed accounts are given in the gospels of the New Testament.

Jesus' last major deed on Earth was the revival of Lazarus from death which widely stirred up a terrific sensation.

Lazarus, being one of the richest landowners of the country, lived in his residence of Bethany not far from Jerusalem, with his two sisters. Friendship with Jesus dated back to the days they first met, years ago. Thereafter, Jesus was welcome to his place whenever he wished to come, to stay any length of time with whomever he was to bring; which, at times, had been hundreds of followers. Always sincerely greeted by the sisters as well, it was a cause for the Temple to spread the defamation that Jesus had an affair with them, especially with Mary. The fact that, in later days, Magdalene lived there too had the rumour mill going even stronger.

Lazarus had his farmlands extensively cultivated by hundreds of labourers, enabling them to earn a fair income to live a decent life with their families. Quite the opposite it was at the Templars' where workers were treated no better than slaves, with the result that nobody wanted to stay there in the end. Many of them had been ruined economically beforehand by evil machinations of the Temple, forcing them to surrender and hire themselves out to their suppressors after totally being indebted. When they found a new home at Lazarus' place their plage ended and none of them ever wanted to go back.

Lazarus, a man of deep religious feelings, respected the old traditions. For many years, a reasonable share of his income was donated by him to the Temple. But he was to witness a loathsome fanaticism more and more taking over and a greed for richness and power. The divine commandments of Moses were replaced by self-proclaimed laws and often reversed to the opposite.

One of the high priests of late, Zechariah, who took a firm stand against corruptness by his moral conduct and chastity, had been murdered while celebrating at the altar. His death was sold to the public as a vanishing in holy ecstasy but many doubted and wondered about it in private.

Lazarus did not actually break with the Temple but the longer the more he had to ward off attempts to wrestle away parts of his properties by juridical tricks or flattery, causing him to withdraw. Yet, the Pharisees, counting on their still high reputation, went in and out his place at will, with ever new claims.

One of their requests was the demand that Lazarus hand over his workforce to them. His answer was to feel free to contact the workers themselves. Which the Pharisees did not even attempt because they knew responses beforehand: Not a single one to accept the deal. So they required the labourers to be transferred by force. Lazarus flatly refused which had him ever the more vilified.

Repercussions to be expected, he remained firm in the cause, counting on the real rulers of the country, the Romans. Had he not been in negotiations with them, asking for their protection, things might have been worse.

What especially embittered him was the intrusiveness he was exposed to by unwelcome visits of the Pharisees at his premises any time they felt like it. Until it reached the point of not being tolerable any longer and measures be taken to end the nuisance once and for all.

Jesus had been aware of the problem and solved

it by supplying Lazarus with a pack of huge dogs which, strolling around the place, behaved meek as lambs. But with any Pharisee in sight they turned into raging beasts. Only once the intruders had to be confronted with them to learn the lesson. The temple-guards, a sort of private army accompanying them for defence, proved to be of no use. When attacked by the dogs, they were running even faster than their masters. So they finally stayed away.

Calm was restored and no more physical interference of the intruders to be feared, yet, all the more so their woven webs of intrigues. Their spreading of defamation was poisonous like corroding fumes. They filed lawsuits in Roman courts against Lazarus, constructing lies and phony accusations. Winning all juridical fighting, Lazarus outwardly appeared to stay calm and self-controlled, but the constant attacks undermined his peace of mind and, subsequently, his physical health.

The Temple's elders must have had a keen sense of the deteriorating situation and kept going at it. The more malicious and baseless the attacks, the deeper they struck inwardly. Lazarus had been warned about it by Jesus but his soul was not made to cope with the ongoing psychic terror. A borderline being crossed, he could not bear it any longer and fell ill with a fierce fever.

The sisters were highly alarmed. It was not only the care for their beloved brother but the concern for their entire physical existence that worried them. Not only were their own lives affected, but the continuation of everyone's living at the premises was at stake if the ailing should die. With no male inheritor, one third of the enterprise would go to the Temple in accordance to the country's laws. As fate had it, there neither were brothers nor cousins nor any other male descendents.

Even worse: The Temple was authorised to take the family's female members in custody when without male protection, with the prospect that they never would escape their harsh regime when being captives behind the Temple's walls. So the scenario unfolded that the other two thirds of the property got lost as well, all sorts of values and servants, staff and workforce included, to be at free disposal of new owners. To the Temple a very promising perspective, indeed.

In red alert it was send for Jesus. But nobody knew his whereabouts. So the illness took its course, fate could not be averted and Lazarus died. Mourning and misery was heart-rending beyond bearing.

All the time Jesus, without intervening, perceived in spirit the going-on. To the disciples, he mentioned the illness in a way they were not really worried because they trusted, should it be necessary, his ability to heal. When he said Lazarus was sleeping but he would not wake him up yet, they were not alarmed. Only when they explicitly heard of the friend's death, it was a shock to them. Jesus for all his almightiness – could he not have prevented the worst? Was there still hope? Hadn't they seen the friend just a while ago sound and safe? Maybe it was no cruel reality that Lazarus' passed away but that he was in a state of being seemingly dead only?

Jesus neither responded to the disciples' mumblings of grief nor to anxious questions. The way proceedings went was the way he wanted them to be, to round off his days on Earth by a final demonstration of his divine might. Several days Lazarus was laying in his grave and only then Jesus left for Bethany, beckoning his followers to come with him as witnesses.

Arriving at the family estate, they were confronted with grief and sorrow. Martha, weeping and heartbroken, said: „Lord, if thou hadst been here my brother had not died." Her sister Mary, hiding among her close friends, was called and she rushed to where Jesus was.

She fell down to his feet, sobbing out of grief and joy of rcunion alike, not able to utter a single word. Until he lifted her from the ground and held her in his arms, saying to the unconsolable that her brother well could have been saved had she only stood firm in unfaltering faith to God when overwhelmed by doubt and anxiety.

Tears of compassion in their eyes, the bystanders betrayed by their looks that they too did not understand the cruelty of fate. Noticing it, Jesus' reaction was as stated in New Testament: „Jesus groaned in the spirit, and was troubled", and „he wept".

He wept out of sadness over their still weak faith. The miracles they either had heard of or witnessed with their own eyes – the memory of it was extinct by the magnitude of grief and lament in heart-rending sorrow. Mary, drowned in her feelings, was crying bitterly.

Jesus asked: „Where have ye laid him?", and they said: „Lord, come and see". Mary dried her tears and showed the way as if he who knew all the roads of the world ever was in need of a guide. Again he wept and people around thought it was for the love of the deceased only.

The grave, located in a hollow at the end of a cavern driven into a wall of rocks, was covered by a heavy tombstone. To labourers working nearby Jesus said: „Take ye away the stone!". They disbelievingly looked at Martha who tried to explain their hesitation: „Lord, by this time he stinketh for he hath been dead four days".

Again, Jesus issued a firm command and with great effort the stone was lifted to the side. Everyone drew back at once because of the horrendous stench that came out of the grave.

Jesus stood in front of the tomb, prayed to his father in heaven and then called with a loud voice: „Lazarus, come forth!" The evil stench vanished all in a moment. Martha and Mary, caught between doubt and a faint hope already stirring up their minds when walking to the tomb, breathlessly watched the unfolding scene in front of their eyes.

Suddenly both rushed forwards with loud outcries of awe and joy: Still covered with sheets of cerement, hand and foot bound all over, Lazarus arose. While the sisters helped to loosen them to let him go free, the crowd outside the tomb shyly withdrew from Jesus when he came out.

The time it happened, no Pharisees were present. Hearing of Lazarus' death, first thing they did had been to fan out for the take-over of the place. At long last! Their strategy had paid off! Together with the temple-guards, they swarmed over land and premises, hardly to respect private spheres of the sisters any longer whom they lecherously eyed. The big guardian dogs listlessly laid around, never to stir at the intruders raid.

What especially made the priests triumph was the prospect that external estates like Lazarus' big guest-house at the Mount of Olives were theirs now. A thorn in their flesh that they never had a chance to get hold of it, they now were more than pleased the way the issue was settled. As assumed new proprietors, they immediately invited all associates to the place to join the celebration of their victory.

The caretaker of the house was ordered to open gates and doors, kitchens and cellars. Wine was poured out to everyone like water. Even the harsh temple-guards got their share to keep them in good temper for further actions while their masters sett-led juridical details.

In the midst of the festivities the news exploded of what happened in Bethany. The first moment no-one was to believe it. Even afterwards they never did. Their sole explanation was a deception of monstrous dimensions. Either Lazarus had not died at all, everything being a dirty fake, or a body double was acting in his name. Whatever the case, it was nothing but outrageous, vicious fraud!

Instantly an assembly was called for counter-measures to be taken. But among all the clamour for revenge rational voices were heard: East of River Jordan, a desert region was said to have trans-formed to fertile, fruit-bearing stretches of land after its poor inhabitants affectionately had welcomed Jesus when visiting the place. Was it done by divine power? Would they not fare better to accept the facts and arrange with him who was able to perform such deeds?

The voice of sanity got lost, met by the majority's furious uproar: It was nothing but fraud, evil fraud, soon to be uncovered! The assembly overwhelming-ly voted for putting an end to it right away, at any cost.

With the temple-guards already at hand, up and away they went to Bethany, all together. The plan was to lure Lazarus, be it the genuine one or the faked, into the open and the magician Jesus as well. And then strike and hit hard and no mercy what-soever!

At first, the action seemed to go well but as soon as they arrived at Bethany things went spinning out of control: The huge dogs, guardians of the place again, awoke to furious life and pounced upon the intruders. No matter how many they were, armed to the teeth, nobody dared a single move. Who tried nonetheless, was not standing on his feet for long, lucky to get away alive, though not without scars.

To the Pharisees, it was a shock as never there had been one in their lives. Lazarus – it was him, indeed – came and stood there, just eyeing them. It was not much he had to say but Jesus, accompanying him, said all the more. Urging the wrongdoers to change their lives for the better, he pointed to the evil outcome of all further lies and misdoings if carrying on. Yet, it was in vain.

But to listen they had, teeth grinding, whether they wanted or not. Thereafter, the dogs were signalled to do their job. Within no time, all were in a desperate hurry to dart off as fast as they could, the dogs on their backs, furiously snarling.

The people of Bethany which shyly had withdrawn from the scene when eye-witnessing Lazarus' revival, felt small. In the presence of divine power they deemed themselves mere sinners, shivering how ever to stand ground in the event's awesome and scaring light.

But Jesus approached them and revealed, in a soft voice, the real cause of their fear: It was their priests' lifelong insinuation to imagine God as a God of vengeance and retaliation ever to be worshipped in fear of punishment for sinning, to have them shake and tremble forever. In spheres infinitely high above he was to reside, never to forgive neglect of service by them, poor sinners as they were.

How much they were mistaken! In truth it was

the opposite: He, who came in lovingness and charity, wanted nothing but to show the path to unending life, not damnation. If they ever were to wake up to realize it! Like Lazarus had done: „My Lord and my Saviour!", he had exclaimed, falling down to his knees when becoming a living man again. Jesus had lifted him up in his arms and they hugged like one brother the other.

The dwellers of Bethany, when watching, eventually shed their shyness and joyfully surrounded their saviour. Saviour to them in a very substantial way: For no-one ever was to imagine a life under the rule of the Temple, taking over the place, without having shivers going down his spine.

To restore full health, Lazarus strengthened himself with bread and wine and gave order to arrange for a great feast, a long-standing tradition at joyful events with everyone being invited, neighbours and all. But Jesus hinted that many, many more were to be expected than was thought in the first place, well-wishers from nearby Jerusalem who had known and loved Lazarus. After the news spread they set out for Bethany to express their great joy, a crowd of over a thousand.

Even though Lazarus' place was equipped at its best, the residents were overstrained by the task, lacking facilities for so many people. It was not the time for miracles any longer – things were to be done by men themselves – but one had to be asked able to cope with the immense request: Angel Raphael.

In the blink of an eye he could have provided the necessities for the thousand guests, the meals prepared and the wine supplied. But he rather solved the problem by putting the hands of the many willing helpers at work. To every problem he knew an answer and in an atmosphere of excitement in kitchens and guest-rooms there was bustling activity. Missing items were found in time even when nobody really knew how. Within an hour the tables were set with exquisite delicacies for the many visitors and everyone was highly pleased with the succeedings, without pondering much about special feelings of miracles.

The guests arrived and were seated. But prior to the beginning of the festivities all of them praised and thanked Him who by his unheard-of deed had been the initiator of their gathering.

The day's proceedings significantly promoted their common cause when the disciples mingled with the guests, lecturing them about new ways of living in mutual understanding and love of God as taught by Jesus. Replacing the degenerated religious rules of the Temple, it trustfully was received by the public and got known throughout the country.

To the scribes and elders it was extremely disturbing. Being short of one last spark, the raging flames of wrath were fanned to full blaze.

15. Blind Commotion

To take revenge for Lazarus' outrageous deceit all members of the Temple were summoned again to a general assembly to be sworn in to eternal hate. Yet, things were not all that smooth the way they were running. Some high-ranking Templars would no longer deny what they had seen with their own eyes or heard from trustworthy witnesses. But their view was hooted down by the majority: Fraud, malicious fraud, all of it! Anything linked to these hell-raisers was nothing but infamous deception to build up hostile opposition to the Temple! One way or the other, it was absolutely vital to put an end to it!

Especially to this Jesus! But how to get hold of him? The attack by the hounds of hell still chilled them to the bones. Besides, they had to face another problem: The Romans! Jesus had powerful friends among them, protecting him.

They pondered over triggering a defamation campaign to accuse him of open rebellion for regime change, countrywide. The plain folk, was it not shouting for to make him their king? Rather today than tomorrow the Templars were to carry out their evil intentions but for the moment nothing could be done except to hold out and wait for the right occasion.

Lazarus was blacklisted as well by them, especially for his part of having so many people turned away from the Temple, all of them believers now of the new faith – a trend gaining momentum by the hour if not stopped! But he felt not really alarmed, unshakeable now the way he was. He knew he was protected by his divine Lord, and by the dogs, if ever there was an assault.

Knowing the end of his mission on Earth drawing near, Jesus prepared to retreat to hidden places to spend his time in contemplation. To become human to full extent he had to renounce all divine power. He, the Creator, was to unite with the created forever by sharing with them what they suffered on Earth and dreaded most: Death! To him, a very cruel death as he foresaw only to well.

Lazarus, instead, rather hoped to have him as a guest in the oncoming winter. Hints given by Jesus about his fate still being beyond understanding to him, he anxiously exclaimed: „Lord, you certainly will not succumb to this brute, worth only to be obliterated forever!?"

When Jesus talked about the inevitable to the disciples, the sheer thought of surrender to the Temple appeared an absurdity to them, too. Having witnessed his almightiness so often, their brains registered the words but their hearts revolted.

In wintertime, before leaving for their retreat, Jesus left it to his numerous followers to stay with him or settle their private affairs back home. Most of them accepted the latter, while the inner circle of the future apostles decided to come, except for Judas Iscariot.

Judas had been very impressed by the events happening at Bethany which definitely convinced him of God's Kingdom to be erected soon. To this effect, he was willing to do everything he could to help the project along, hoping for an appropriate position once it materialized. Activities, skilfully unfurled by him, seemed to advance the matter. He was seen and heard in the town of Jericho delivering passionate speeches in front of masses of inhabitants to speed up the coming incidents.

Jericho was the winter residence of King Herod. Judas' activities soon attracted his attention. By constantly raising quarrels with the Romans, same as he did with the Temple, Herod was trying to extend his sphere of influence. This fabulous saint Jesus, Judas was rattling about, possibly could be helpful in promoting his affairs, he reckoned.

Besides, persuasiveness and deceit of a woman had caused Herod to order the disgraceful beheading of John, the Baptiser, and ever since it burdened his conscience. John, as „the voice crying in the wilderness", had been of great influence to the public when he heralded new times to come. (John, the baptiser, son of the high priest Zechariah who once was murdered at the Temple's altar, is not to be confused with John, the disciple and future evangelist, whom Jesus loved.)

Superstitious as he was, Herod much regretted the murder afterwards for fear of John's spirit taking revenge on him from the world beyond. Obsessed by the idea to have coming mischief averted grace to the supernatural power of this widely-known Jesus, Herod hoped to be introduced to him by Judas.

Judas, for his part, thought King Herod useful in pursuing his ardent ambitions of a future takeover by Lord Jesus, speculating for desired positions in the coming system.

Accordingly, he felt flattered when invited to Herod's court, to a network of stealth in whose intrigues he soon found himself entangled. Furthermore, he preached to the masses in public places, promising heaven on Earth, hinting liberation from the rules of oppressors. He was not overtly naming names but it easily was guessed whom he meant.

The Romans! He did not bear in mind that some of the truest friends ever of Jesus were among them, like Cyrenius. Yet, Cyrenius unendingly was engaged in matters of governance in far-away Tyros at the Mediterranean coast and had no perception of what was going on, while in Jerusalem, in a subordinate position, Pontius Pilate was residing as proconsul and ruler of the city thanks to his aristocratic birthright, trying not to get into troubles too much, neither with the defiant Herod nor with the Temple.

Judas hoped to be a player in the ongoing political theatre. His visions – and the drive to get them materialized – gradually were taking shape in his overheated brain. It led to the act eternally remembered and linked to his name: The betrayal – Judas' attempt to force a seemingly reluctant Jesus to demonstrate his almightiness and seize power of the world. For his misjudgment he dearly had to pay, with his life. Jesus once hinted, Judas was not exactly an evil character but one torn apart by inner discrepancies and ambitions.

Springtime approaching, Lazarus longingly waited for Jesus' return, not least because he hoped for help against the ever increasing intrigues of the Temple's elders, threatening him with eternal execration and damnation. He suspected they even would try to poison him, once they figured out how.

To find the winter lodging of the disciples and their master, a messenger was send to a remote mountain region in the wilderness where the looked-for were thought to have established themselves, living in derelict ruins of old castles, reasonably repaired against the strong cold of the winter.

Having found Jesus after searching long and wide, he returned with a message which caused Lazarus to seek the protection of the Romans and definitely break with the Templars, putting an end to all their speculations concerning his properties and premises. The Temple, once being the highest religious authority to him, had lost all credit.

When Easter time drew near, Lazarus, from an overlook, kept watching the roads running up from the south for signs of the eagerly awaited friend's arrival. At long last he espied the oncoming company and had them welcomed most heartily. To everyone's joy they finally were back, although Peter, the disciple, strongly had voted against returning, fearing some sort of ambush by the Temple. But Jesus had told him not to interfere with his divine mission.

The days to follow saw the disciples' gathering with their master in bigger or smaller groups, listening to lectures about spiritual and social life, as found in the gospels of the New Testament. But certain remarks they could not decipher, their meaning remained dark and menacing as if foreboding hard times ahead.

All of a sudden Judas reappeared. While the disciples struggled to get over their feelings of discomfort, he eloquently started ranting about events definitely to happen soon: Short of the one spark to set the world on fire, everything was ready to inflame people to sweep away the old system! The magic of his words had a quality to overwhelm listeners against their own will.

But when Jesus came silence set in, great with expectation. Solemnly, he spoke words about the fulfilment of his mission, about elevation, of being „raised". While they stayed cryptic to the disciples, not knowing what to make out of it, Judas interpreted them his own way, never suspecting that their meaning was substantially different from what he thought.

They were assembled in the hall when the door opened. In came Mary, sister of Lazarus. She performed an act which ever since is remembered as the 'Anointment in Bethany', but later-on was confused with a similar deed by Mary Magdalene.

Not looking left or right, she went straight up to Jesus, knelt to the floor before him and, weeping loudly, covered his feet with kisses. „Then took Mary a pound of ointment of spikenard, very costly, and anointed the feet of Jesus, and wiped his feet with her hair, and the house was filled with the odour of the ointment", says the bible. It was an act of utmost grandeur, solely to be performed at the inauguration of kings.

Judas, self-appointed head of finance, could not help but comment on it as squandering, complaining the ointment being worth a fortune, three hundred pence at least. Why for heavens sake was it not given to the hungry poor? It easily would sell for that! To the other disciples it just was one more confirmation of his known greediness making him talk like this, well-nourished as he was.

Jesus answered – and to some it appeared another subtle hint that their master soon was to leave them – „Let her be alone, against the day of my burying hath she kept this. For the poor always ye have with ye; but me ye have not always." Saying this, he lifted the heart-broken sobbing young woman from the floor and blessed and comforted her.

Later on, it was Peter asking Jesus if he ever had in mind to preach to the crowd in the Temple, vigorously trying to argue against it. Because their return had not passed unnoticed. The Temple's spies were hanging around everywhere, mingling with folks, and their spiteful looks did not forebode anything good.

But Jesus commanded him to stay calm. Nobody was to hinder what he had to do: The fulfilment of his mission on Earth!

Lurking, Judas overheard the words and again interpreted them his way. Secretly triumphing, he got up and left the company. The great chance finally had come and he was ready to execute what he thought was his task.

Throughout the city he started pulling strings of connections already in existence, being on the move to collect data and passing them on. Due to the forthcoming festivities, the capital brimmed over with visitors, many of whom solely had come to see the fabulous magician. The news were spreading fast: Up to the Temple! Jesus will deliver a fundamental speech tomorrow!

Triumphantly riding into the city on a burrow's colt the next day, Palm Sunday, it was what the Bible describes as the Coming of Jesus to Jerusalem. A large crowd of thousands, mobilized by Judas and companions, already waited outside the gates, honouring and cherishing Jesus by covering the streets with strewn branches of palm trees – since times of old the ceremony of salutation at the coronation of a king. When the crowd recognised Lazarus accompanying Jesus, jubilation and rejoicing went on unendingly.

Who did not rejoice were the elders of the Temple, the rallying and shouting in the city as an ugly ringing in their ears. Feeling like walking on thin ice, crushing any moment, they preferred to disappear, no traces of them to be found any more for the time being.

Ready to break any resistance in their ecstasy, the masses moved towards the Temple. Yet, there was nothing left to break. All doors and gateways were swung wide open, even of the innermost sanctuary which only the High Priest himself was allowed to enter.

The complete absence of the priests was highly irritating because the great idea, popping up in peoples' minds, could not be executed and fulfilled without them. The plan was to proclaim and enthrone Jesus as king although nobody, except for a few, really knew where the idea suddenly had come from. But, for a coronation to be an irrevocable fact, it had to be done by the High Priests, applying the Holy Ointment on the king-to-be, the holy oil they guarded in their treasuries. They were to do it, definitely, even if prompted by sheer force! Patrols fanned out in search for them, but it was in vain. Where ever there went, the priests had vanished into thin air.

The sellers and buyers, however, who along with the moneychangers had their businesses spread out in the Temple again, hastily cleared up and left the place in remembrance of bygone calamities.

By lack of further action, the surge of emotions somewhat cooled down and all eyes were focused on Jesus when he paced his way into the Temple, followed by the would-be insurrectionists. The ample hall filled with the large masses, still expecting some sort of marvellous happening resulting in ultimate glory.

Jesus entered the open sanctuary, to plain folk a capital crime even to go near. Stepping up to the altar, he turned around and faced the immense crowd. Everyone breathlessly waited for the word, the one word that was to set things in motion even without the priests, the spark to set the world on fire and sweep away the existing regime by calling for revolution.

With a loud and clear voice Jesus spoke. But what he said was entirely different from what was expected. He said that from now on no altars were to be erected in temples of any kind other than inside the heart of every human. Solely there the true altar was, by obeying the commandments of loving God and loving one another. No hate, no quarrelling, no want to dominate others! Then, and only then, a kingdom could evolve in which everyone would have a fair share.

To emphasize what he meant he turned to the many sick and ailing, occupying the space alongside the walls of the Temple, a great deal of them already waiting for ages. They waited for healing be granted by God, arranged by the priest's petitionary prayers, provided appropriate payment be done beforehand. When everything proved to be ineffective and the last financial resources gone while the sick still were left in their misery – well, then it was their own fault, the failing probably due to impure thoughts during the priest's prayers!

Recognizing the hopes and cravings for healing, Jesus addressed the deceived and in view of the masses, standing close to each other in the wide hall, he granted what they were longing for: Health – health to all of them, the lame and the crippled, the blind and the deaf, even to those with missing limbs – in a single moment they were sound and unscathed. Loudly they praised the Lord Almighty.

The waiting crowd's reaction was mixed. Once again jubilation erupted, yet, those yelling for king and kingdom were disappointed. Healing, so what? Things the like already were known of Jesus, almost being normal, even if the strange way they were effectuated was not quite clear. But what the crowd really wanted, more than anything in the world, was something different: A king of might and glory, so bright and brilliant that they themselves could be a part of the glory and splendidness as well.

The turning of the general mood did not pass un-heeded. In disguise, the Temple's spies mingled with the people and did their best to downplay the healing and upgrade the escalating uneasiness: This quack of Nazareth – his pretensions and cryptic promises, would it not finally turn out to be a tremendous deception? So went the hissing, and the bawlers for kingdom grew uncertain about what they wanted.

All the more so, since Jesus called with a loud voice that the installation of a kingdom, demanded by a bawling populace in their lust for greatness, always had resulted in disaster in the past, ending in havoc, in wars and conflicts and subsequently in bloodshed and captivity. Was that what they really desired?

Old King Herod who panicked for the rumour of a new born child, suspected to be a future rival, opting for mass murder of the children of the land as counter-measures – what did they think would the new Herod's reaction be at the prospect of a competitor for the throne? If they ever wished for civil war and unending bloodshed, they just were to carry on!

His reasoning not taken seriously, Jesus' words remained unheeded. The bawlers more and more grew convinced they had been following the wrong one. What they spotted was not the shining hero they had wished for, longing for glory. When Jesus called out to the people, „my kingdom is not of this world", the temper of the crowd toppled over altogether.

16. The Rising

The proceedings look like steadily drifting towards disaster while in truth they were the preliminary of the greatest deed ever done for mankind. Judas had no inkling of his own significance, yet he was the medium for events to happen the way they did.

To him, the outcome of the day had been a complete calamity. Early morning's high spirits, when a huge crowd was marching towards success, he as one of the players pulling the strings behind the scene, had given way to the abominable feeling of utter failure.

The moment the general mood so quickly had changed, the initiative instantly was seized by the Temple. Without delay, horn-blowers were heralding a Ministry of Reconciliation, ordered by God Almighty himself, for the purpose of general absolution and forgiveness of sins to benefit everyone attending.

Celebrated in splendid ostentation, the masses, just about a short while ago bawling for a king, were drawn to it like under a spell. The Temple's well-known greed changed to gorgeous generosity. Magnificent feasting and donations to the poor were launched and did not fail to generate the desired impact: By the double-minded, the to-be king soon was forgotten. Those who did not forget silently went away, having no voice to be heard in the upsurge of insanity. Furthermore, the Temple had its mockery spread of Jesus having said „The son of man must rise". The words, having a twofold meaning no-one understood, were ridiculed as pure nonsense.

Realizing everything said by him being twisted and perverted, Jesus silently turned away and left. The host of the disciples, too, took to the road home to Bethany, deeply in thought about what had gone wrong. What in the beginning appeared to be a final blow against the Temple Jesus had in mind to strike, inexplicably ended in total failure. His former power, did all of it had left him?

In Bethany, Jesus in solitude retreated to a quiet place while the others still were engaged in long-winding discussions. Especially Judas hardly was able to control his agitated emotions when talking about his frustration in a way it almost scared his companions.

He was not to doubt Jesus' divine power, he said, but it lived in a physical body still to weak for the task to be done. In last decisive moments what could have led to overall success was ruined by his meekness. „It is not meekness and gentleness alone the world is ruled by. It also is the hand able to bear the sword and, if it must be, is prepared to strike in rigorous severity", was his statement, voicing the principles of the world as it was.

That Jesus incarnated to help and enlighten human beings was beyond his grasp. The others intuitively understood and sensed what was meant. „The Lord certainly knows best his plans and doings", Peter, the disciple, firmly said. Whereafter Judas fell silent, gloomily brooding for the rest of the night.

What had it been going wrong? Short of a last blow, the Lord could have scored full success! Why was he so faint-hearted and hesitant, missing out on a golden opportunity instead of seizing it? The final triumph almost being within reach, why must he have bothered with the sick and crippled? The nation as a whole, was it not of infinite higher priority? The firm and the strong, for so long gnashing their teeth in anger of the Temple's oppression – and likewise the slavery by a foreign military power, pressing heavy taxes from them, squandering it all in luxury in far-away Rome, – did they not deserve any better?

A faint hint solely, given at the right moment, and everyone would have been ready for the uprising to sweep away tyranny and replace it by a kingdom of power and glory, paradise on earth, governed by a righteous ruler to transform sorrow into happiness and poverty into abundance – and the hint had not come! Yet, at countless occasions before, had Jesus not demonstrated his power so very clearly? Overshadowed by divine might like never a man before, he definitely had the strength to turn things around. Why for heaven's sake, why did he always shy away from action when it came to the last step!? Judas' thoughts spun round and round in a circle, returning to the same odd riddle again and again.

He tried to talk about it to his old companion Thomas who, too, had to fight off lurking doubt. But what Judas was pondering over frightened him. Especially when he said, the Lord, if he did not dare to take the last and final step by himself, he must be forced to!

Be forced? The Lord, ruler of the universe and master of countless hosts of angels – be forced? Thomas was shaken to the core. Judas, had he not seen with his own eyes Angel Raphael who called himself the least and lowest servant of God, when demonstrating but a trifle of his power that could have shattered the world? No-one on Earth was to force anything upon Raphael, let alone upon Jesus! How could one even think of it? „Brother, refrain from it, it is of no good. I dread it, it's a horror!"

As an answer, Judas muttered something under his breath like Thomas being a coward and weakling, yet made him promise to keep silence about what was said. Then he withdrew to mull over what had been on his mind so many times before. He did not exactly know how to start, but things had to take their course, he felt, one way or the other.

It was the moment the plan irrevocably took shape in his brain which in its monstrosity he had not dared to really think about in detail, nor about its consequences: To render the Lord into the hands of the torturers and have his life threatened by their brutal force.

Then, finally, Jesus would have to bring into action his divine power as a definite Must if he and his mission were not miserably to perish. It could not turn out any other way! Absolutely not!

The outcome is described in all the four gospels of the Bible: The Betrayal of Jesus! The impression might arise that Judas was motivated by greed because he was paid thirty pieces of silver by the Temple. Being Judas, he did not reject them, but the true motivation, as the 'Great Gospel of John' assures us, was his craving for power he hoped to share when things would turn out his way.

Yet, the money he took was blood-money and not before long it was to torch him like fire in hell and let his soul cringe and crumble. As once it was forecast.

While Jesus withdrew to meditate, Judas went on reconnaissance in the city. The Temple still was under surveillance, secured by units of Herod's military, hired for the occasion. Additionally, streets were patrolled by Roman troops, requested from Governor Pilate on grounds to prevent impending insurgencies. Everything stayed calm though, nobody dared to say a word except muttering under the breath.

But Judas was gathering enough information. Everywhere he went, he noticed folks being dismayed: The weird ending of the attempted coup d'etat!

The disappearance of Jesus afterwards! Judas was sure to sense a general mood for a second, this time successful, attempt to overthrow tyranny.

Meanwhile in the Temple, behind closed doors, the priests day and night brooded over the way to capture the insurgent of magical power but all talking produced no result, the failures of the past weighing heavily upon their minds.

Suddenly word came from the gates. Someone outside was demanding admission to deliver a message. It was Judas, as it turned out, and what he had to say concerned his willingness to show the way to apprehend the looked-for. At first, the assembly's reaction had been sheer disbelief but, after giving it a second thought, it was considered to be of some value: In the darkness of the night, when the power of magicians was said to diminish, there indeed might be a reasonable chance to catch them.

They asked Judas, whether he in earnest was prepared to lead them? He was, and the deal was settled. The Pharisees gloated. Location and hour to join up with the temple-guards were arranged to get the mission on its way. Judas saw his plans materialize and deemed himself already a junior regent in an empire of glory.

The further occurrences went on as recorded in the gospels of the Holy Scriptures: The many parables of Jesus' farewell teachings, the ritual eating of the lamb at the feast of the Passover, the washing of the feet of the Twelve as an example to render even lowest services to fellow men, the breaking of the bread and the drinking of the wine – even the 'Great Gospel of John' has not much to add to it.

The disciples still pondered over dark words of betrayal by their master when, during the evening meal, Jesus carried out an act of old tradition. He handed a piece of bread to everyone while citing some line of the scripture. To Judas he said: „What you want to do, do it soon". To the disciples it appeared to be a request for an errand to do, but Judas took it as the demand, even an order, to finally get going with his plan. He silently disappeared; the eagerly awaited hour had come.

The others left as well, setting off for the nearby place of Gethsemane, the beautifully situated garden belonging to Lazarus at the slopes of the Mont of Olives.

It was the place Jesus was to live through the agony of torment in advance, all the cruelties to endure. To fulfil his mission, he had to separate the human part of him from its divine essence. He had to answer the question whether he was prepared to surrender to the pain his enemies were to inflict on him, humiliation and excruciating torture.

The choice was his: To return to divinity and omnipotence to create a world of perfection, an eternal kingdom of splendour and glory in which noone ever was to stray off the path of virtue – or forever affirm men's free will, enabling them to rise to ever greater heights by own efforts, as well as to fathom the deepest abysses of evilness. Abysses Jesus knew he himself had to go through to endure torture no-one was to imagine.

Foreseeing the torment made him say: „My soul is exceeding sorrowful, even unto death", and he begged for the help of his closest disciples: „Tarry je here and watch with me". He was alone with images of horror invading him, attacks of desperation and agony. But, the disciples fell asleep. Three times he made them wake up and three times they went on sleeping.

He fell on his face and prayed, moaning; „O my father, if it be possible, let this cup pass from me: nevertheless not as I will but as thou wilt". And the disciples, barely awoken, he asked why they left him alone in this darkest moments? „Could ye not watch with me one hour?"

Images, stretching into deepest depths, were perceived by Anne Catherine Emmerich, the humble nun, living half a century prior to Lorber. In her visions, when confined to her poor sick-bed, she saw wraiths and demons assaulting Jesus, Satan himself with his hordes of hell.

They screamed it into his ears that it was he himself causing the world's nameless misery, religious wars extinguishing whole populations, cruelties of the inquisition, murder and arson, blood and thunder. Why wasn't he to prevent it? His mere existence alone had been the reason for the bestiality of five thousand innocent children brutally being murdered – all because of him! Eternal shame on him!

He, the creator of the world, who by a whiff could have prevented the evil – but his very own creatures seemingly being of no value to him!

With all the accusations and indictments Jesus twisted and convulsed in pain. When sweat and blood was breaking out of him, he again staggeringly crept to the sleeping disciples. They, driven up in horror, hardly recognized him, his appearance having changed so much for the worse.

The demons returned, pressing Jesus to admit his guilt. They showed him the torture awaiting him if he ever wished to make good for the sins of the world. They maliciously demanded whether he really was to suffer to such an extent, excruciating beyond anything to imagine, on behalf of this ill-bred pack?

Even worse atrocities were to happen in the future when the church, founded by him, destined to be a place of dearest humanity to worship God, was to deteriorate to an abyss of perverted power and idolised false splendour, to evilness of all kind, conflicts and wars devastating whole countries.

Jesus fell to the ground like being destroyed. But inwardly, ever the more, he firmly was prepared to take on responsibility for the world's aberration and to bear all the blame. From heaven an angel appeared and strengthened him. He was willing to endure the oncoming torture in all its bitterness.

It was midnight when a horde of temple-guards, „a great multitude with swords and staves, from the chief priests and the elders of the people", bearing torches, Judas in front of them, drew near. Jesus got up to meet them, the disciples followed. By a kiss, the prearranged sign, Judas revealed to the pursuers who it was they were looking for. Jesus said to him: „Judas, betrayest thou the Son of man with a kiss?"

At first, nobody dared to reach out for the wanted and when Jesus spoke: „Whom seek ye? I am he!", they rebounded and some of them toppled over to the ground by the might of his word.

But then, he allowed to be seized. After overcoming the first shock of horror, realizing Jesus gave in without resistance, even held back the disciples from defending him, the temple-thugs started their mission, carrying it out with brute force. The gospels report they led Jesus to the High Priests and elders. Catherine Emmerich, in her visions, not only saw that they did so, but also the way they did it.

Tying his arms closely to his chest, they fastened ropes to his body and tore him forwards with coarse laughter, deliberately ripping him through debris and thorny brushwoods. When their victim collapsed they brutally dragged him to his feet, only to have him toppling over at next obstacles. At a brook they pushed him in and pulled him through mud and dirt. By sheer luck only, or divine interception, they did not kill him right before reaching their destination.

Getting there, unending humiliation continued, cruelty and torture. Judas, the betrayer, gaping from afar as though betrayed by his own eyes, dashed away in horror.

Contrary to Anne Catherine Emmerich's vision, the „Great Gospel of John", the Lord's autobiography of his time on Earth, states that no report of the excruciating tortures will be given, too much to be understood by living men. The hidden sense of the agony would be revealed only to those of a broader view after having completed life on Earth.

As for the events themselves, they happened as shown in the gospels of the New Testament without hardly anything to be added. Death sentence by the vengeful Templars quickly was pronounced; votes in favour of the convicted were not admitted. Thereafter, as the last step towards execution, the verdict had to be confirmed by the representative of jurisdiction, Roman governor Pilate. But, as it turned out, he refused for reasons of blame unproved.

Meanwhile, a large mob of bawlers, assembled by the Templars, shouted for the sentence to be carried out. „Crucify him, crucify him", they blared. The even larger crowd of people who loved Jesus and wished him well was kept by soldiers at too far a distance for the lamentation and the weeping of the women to be heard.

Pilate did not want to befoul his hands with innocent blood and sent Jesus on to King Herod who curiously was prying to meet the famous magician. But what he saw then was a maltreated creature of misery brought before him with no resemblance left of an alleged mighty wizard. So, being disappointed, he sent Jesus to the thugs of his soldiery who took pleasure to torture him with fierceness of hell. Then they brutally dragged him back to Pilate.

When the inflamed mob, ever the more enraged, continued to blare out „crucify, crucify", Pilate had the baleful idea to arouse the crowd's pity by having Jesus scourged for offences he fraudulently was charged of, as part of the Temple's witch hunt against him. Stripped naked, jeered at by the soldiers, he was hog-tied to a pillar and whipped with thorn-reinforced lashes until the blood ran out and the skin came off in bits. Justice done, Pilate then was to let Jesus go free.

The action produced the opposite effect. The mob went berserk in ever increasing wrath while the Templars threatened to sue Pilate at the emperor's court in Rome as an offender against state laws for not acting on open calls for rebellion by a nation-wide known insurgent. That finally made Pilate to buckle, turning Jesus over to his enemies for the execution to be carried out. Yet prior to it, he did wash his hands in sight of the crowd to demonstrate that he personally was not convinced of any guilt nor did he approve the gruesome proceedings.

Thus the dark words came true about his fate on Earth, Jesus time and again had hinted, which beforehand never really were understood by anyone: That he would be lifted and raised.

A long log of timber and a smaller one at its upper end, forming a cross. On it a man, stretched out and nailed to it though hands and feet, then torn upwards by the barbarous goons until it reached up to the sky and, with its lower end, rattled into a hole in the ground to be wedged and blocked. Above, the representative of mankind, Jesus Christ, Son of God, pierced and speared, sinews ruptured and limbs torn, thirsty and bleeding from countless wounds – that was the rising, prepared for him by his very own creatures. One last word, uttered prior to his soul leaving the body, was: „Father, forgive them because they know not what they do."

Watching from afar in ever increasing horror, Judas Iscariot dashed away, frenzied with fear, and made an end to his life by hanging himself.

The gang of executioners, half drunk as they were, slunk off, task accomplished. The Pharisees in charge of supervising, left in disgust and the Roman soldiers carried on to safeguard the place in silence.

Beneath the cross, mourning in nameless grief, stood Mother Mary and the women of her kin. John, the only disciple never to flee and abandon them, stayed on till all was done and fulfilled, in accordance to divine intentions.

17   Outlook

By his crucifixion and resurrection, Jesus, the Christ and Saviour, vowed to eternally remain united with Earth. Ever since, two millennia passed, times of thriving civilisations aiming at ever more efficiency. But for all the progress, mankind specifically seemed to develop inclinations towards strife and conflict. At whatever corner of the world, fuel was added to flames, and dark powers, whoever they were, commanded the potential to have Earth destroyed by a devastating weaponry, as pointed out by the perpetually spread horror of the media.

Sturdy contemporaries got used to it while more sensitive characters rather hoped for mercy and the good will of a divine lordship to avert disaster. But the Lord, Christ, who made the greatest sacrifice imaginable to advance mankind, would he? Help to preserve the status of today's civilisation?

Traditions and social values as the basis of living-together breaking down, sane human relations and stable communities are not self-evident any longer. Morals, disqualified and abandoned as unscientific leftovers, are substituted by political correctness. Children, from early childhood on, are indoctrinated by perverted views of the world to let them grow up without substantial values, manipulating them by whatever ideology pushed.

The most essential present ever given to mankind, passed on with words as quoted in the Genesis: „Be fruitful and multiply, and replenish the earth" – looks like being largely diverted to lechery. Lust here and there, any time of the day whenever desired, is nuzzled and spread through numerous channels. Presentations bordering on obscenity are especially aimed at young folks to indulge in. Undesired life from sparked activities easily is aborted, posing no problem. Statistics speak volumes and independent minds speak of worldwide murder of unborn life.

Life approaching the other end of the treadmill, if it does not feel like being worth it any longer, is to be disposed of by oneself, sanctioned by law, with professional assistance of experts helping to leave the den of earthly sin. Was that the world, the Creator had in mind when bringing it into existence?

Jesus often warned about conditions getting out of control. Like he did about the rebellion against the Roman empire during the time he lived on Earth. Insurgencies had flared up until they fanned out to the entire country. When the patience of the rulers ran out, the military force of their legions was sent and a once grand civilisation was doomed and its days numbered. Jerusalem, the great city of a million inhabitants, was destroyed and razed to the ground, its foundations hardly to be located in later years. So was the rest of the country.

The bygone fate of those places might not be of much interest nowadays, the prophecies about what is to happen in times ahead should be all the more.

Many statements by Jesus, (given in the years 30 to 33), about future conditions in nearly 2000 year's time – which is the time of today – are found in "The Great Gospel of John", (written 1851 to 1864). Some of them might be translated from a somewhat ancient language as correctly as possible:

„Natural fire will be engaged to do tremendous services. It will propel carriages and ships faster than the wind-storm. Men will learn to tame lightning to make it the fastest messenger of their urges from one end of the world to the other. And when the proud and greedy rulers are waging war against each other, fire will be crucial to execute the task. By its force, the weight of huge masses of iron will be hurled against enemies and their cities to wreak havoc beyond compare."

Given that the statements were made two thousand years ago when technology was non-existent, they are noteworthy as previews of modern war's destructive power. They go along with the deterioration of inner spheres of human minds:

„True faith and love will disappear and give way to delusional beliefs which are generated among the people and forced upon them by all sorts of harassment and punishment. False prophets, ruling in arrogance and selfishness, will claim to be the only true successors and representatives of Mine (Jesus), demanding to be worshipped. And when men, strengthened by my spirit, will arise to fight against the false prophets treasuring gold only, ruling everything by their financial power, there will be war and persecution the world has not seen since the beginning of time."

Yet, the citations end with a promise: „But these darkest states of affairs will not go on for long and it shall come to pass that the dark rulers will sound the death bells for themselves. Because the spirit of trueness will be awoken among the people being so hard-pressed in many ways ..."

Whatever to think of these statements – there are many similar ones – times ahead will be rough. Yet, the gloom and the darkness is nothing but the shadow cast by the light. The deeper the shadow the brighter the light at the other side. It just needs to be looked for.

In the beginning it may be a mere gleam only but it will grow. It will foster the motivation not to give up until the way is found out of the darkness. And then, almost blinded by light, to recognize someone standing in front of us at the other side: Jesus, the Christ, patiently waiting.

He waits for us to come to him, regarding him not only as the almighty ruler but the brother who longs to meet his earthly brothers and sisters. To look out for us, continually has been his intention since the world began and the creation brought into being.

„A heart which truly and sincerely loves me, is a gift to me greater than heaven and earth with all their riches and glory!", are the words he gave to humanity when promising to help. They will remain, even with changes to come no living man is able to fully comprehend today.

At times, the Lord commemorates himself. Occurrences come about no one ever anticipated, resulting in social turmoil that turns life upside down. He not deliberately has them to happen but rather allows them, self-made by men as they are, as nudges to remind people of the consequences of aberration from the path of truth in a world that widely has forgotten him.

As the Lord of the time, a thousand years are to him but a wink of an eye, and all of eternity is to his command for the guidance of men, his very own creatures. If they ever long for it.

*   *   *

The „Great Gospel of John", existing in addition to the four gospels of the New Testament, is translated into English, yet might not easily be understood. Like it is the case with the original version, given roughly two centuries ago in an antiquated German language. It was the language of the time, a beautiful one for sure, but definitely not what widely is in use today.

With hardly any room left for a sense of spirituality, the meaning of terms and phrases shifted by altered definitions and the orientation towards the needs for effectiveness of the modern world. Reading about the events of old and their true meaning, requires effort but the gains might be immeasurable for those who truly believe. After all, they are God's own words.

The novel tries to show a tiny fraction of the original contents. Its five thousand pages that came into being in the past, were hidden to the world for a long time. Secrecy had been vital as a protective measure against an omnipotent church which suppressed, confiscated and destroyed every trace of aberration from official doctrines of faith, especially since the text contained many quotations about the pious institution's display of worldly power when inner truth was abandoned in favour of political goals.

A small circle of friends surrounded Jakob Lorber during the years he, by grace of the Lord, received the Inner Word. They helped to preserve it for times to come. After Lorber died, the messages were passed on to followers, engaged to get them more widely known once the church had lost its dominance. Edited and published in the course of time, they eventually became available to anyone who wished for them.

Whether they made it to broad public attention is another question. For the time being, they rather look like being buried beneath worldly vanities. Yet, they are not lost. In ages ahead, they will be highly valued as the Lord's genuine words.

Bible quotations are taken from the
King James Version
Other quotations are from the
Great Gospel of John